"O come, let us worship and bow down;
Let us kneel before the LORD our maker."
Psalm 95:6

PSALMS

Books 4 & 5

Psalms 90 - 150

Lucian Farrar, Jr.

James Kay Publishing

Tulsa, Oklahoma

Psalms
Books 4 & 5
ISBN 978-1-943245-79-6

www.jameskaypublishing.com

e-mail: sales@jameskaypublishing.com

Cover design by JKP
Cover Graphic courtesy of World Video Bible School
www.wvbs.org
Author Photo by Bob Cooper

also by
Lucian Farrar, Jr.

The Victorious Church
In the Book of Revelation
A Commentary and Questions

The Book of Daniel
The Most High Rules
A Commentary and Questions

The Minor Prophets
God's Spokesmen
A Commentary and Questions

The Book of Isaiah
Christ, Our Redeemer
A Commentary and Questions

The Life of Christ
A Chronological Account

Psalms
Book 1
David's Original Collection

Psalms
Books 2 & 3
Psalms 42 - 89

Dedication

This book is dedicated to my son-in-law,

Norman Jones

Norman is a dedicated Christian, an outstanding Bible teacher and song leader. He preaches when needed, and he now serves as an elder. Norman wrote a song for my sister when she was nearing death. I treasure his song, *"Waiting on Angels to Carry Her Away."* I am thankful that Norman is the husband of my daughter, Melisa.

— Lucian Farrar, Jr.

Thank you,
    To Bob Colvin for proofreading this book.

The King James Version is used for the most part in this book. At times, archaic word endings have been deleted for clarity. Whenever verbs are before the subject of a declarative sentence, the word order has been changed to avoid being misunderstood as a question. Present-day punctuations have been used. Changes also have been made in format to indicate parallelism.

Other translations are acknowledged
by the following abbreviations:

ESV – English Standard Version
NASB – New American Standard Bible, 1973
NIV – New International Version, 1996
NKJV – New King James Version, 1996

These translations are used to replace archaic words with those that can be understood today or to give a more accurate meaning of the original text.

Table of Contents

PSALMS

Book Four

Psalms of Praise

Psalms 90 – 106

The collection of these psalms of praise may have begun during Hezekiah's reign. As king, he restored the worship of the LORD in the temple. He "commanded the Levites to sing praises to the LORD with the words of David and of Asaph the seer." (2 Chronicles 29:30)

Psalm 106 was written after the Jews were exiled in Babylon because we read in verse forty-six, "He made them also to be pitied of all those that carried them captives." Other psalms in Book Four were written after the Jews returned to Jerusalem after their exile.

Psalm 90

God's Eternity and Man's Frailty

A Prayer of Moses, the man of God

This psalm by Moses is similar to the Song of Moses in Deuteronomy 32. God's eternal existence and power are praised in Psalm 90:1-2. Man's brief existence on the earth is lamented in verses 3-6. The punishment for sins is described in verses 7-11. The psalm concludes with a prayer for our hearts to be guided by God's wisdom and for God's mercy to be upon us. (12-17)

> **LORD, you have been our dwelling place**
> **in all generations.**
> **Before the mountains were brought forth**
> **or ever you had formed the earth and the world,**
> **even from everlasting to everlasting,**
> **You are God. 90:1-2**

The LORD is our home providing love and comfort and food and protection. When Moses wrote this psalm, the Israelites were wandering in the wilderness without a permanent house in which to live; they were living in tents and were constantly moving from one place to another. But God was with them, providing for all their needs. When they got hungry, he fed them with bread from heaven. When they got thirsty, he gave them water from the rock. He even kept their clothing and shoes from wearing out. (Deut. 29:5)

Jesus tells us that our heavenly Father knows our needs. If we seek first God and his righteousness, he will provide for us. (Matthew 6:31-33) God will help us as he helped Israel. But at times, he made them do without things they needed, to remind them that he is the source of blessings. The apostle Paul also learned this lesson. (Philippians 4:11-13) God is our home.

We should worship and serve the LORD our God. He is eternal. He has no beginning and no end. He is the Creator of all things, both in the heavens and in the earth.

> **You turn man to destruction; and say,**
> **"Return, ye children of men."**
> **For a thousand years in your sight**
> **are but as yesterday when it is past,**
> **and as a watch in the night.**
> **You carry them away with a flood;**
> **They are as a sleep.**
> **In the morning they are like grass which grows up.**
> **In the morning, it flourishes and grows up;**
> **In the evening, it is cut down and withers. 90:3-6**

God formed man of the dust of the ground; and he said, "And to dust you shall return." (Genesis 2:7; 3:19) Before the flood, men lived almost a thousand years; but with God, a thousand years are as one day or just a few hours in the night. Time is nothing with God; for everyone is soon swept away as by a flood. Our lives are like a dream when we sleep. We are like the grass that thrives in the spring and early summer and withers and dies in the fall.

> **For we are consumed by your anger,**
> **and by your wrath we are troubled.**
> **You have set our iniquities before you,**
> **our secret sins in the light of your countenance.**
> **For all our days are passed away in your wrath;**
> **We spend our years as a tale that is told.**
> **The days of our years are seventy years;**
> **And if by reason of strength they are eighty years,**
> **yet their strength is labor and sorrow;**
> **for it is soon cut off, and we fly away.**
> **Who knows the power of your anger?**
> **Even according to your fear, so is your wrath.**
> **90:7-11**

The LORD was angry with the people of Israel who complained that he had brought them to the land of Canaan to fall by the sword; and they wanted to return to Egypt as slaves. God said that those who complained against him would die in the wilderness, "from twenty years old and above." (Numbers 14:29) God will also be angry with us if we refuse to follow Jesus our Redeemer into Heaven, our land of promise. When hardships come, some Christians return to the slavery of sin. We cannot hide our sins from God's face. (Hebrews 4:12-13)

Our lives are like a story that is told, with a beginning and an end. Even if we live to be eighty years old, it seems like a short time. Some think that Moses could not be the writer of this psalm because he lived to be 120 years old. However, God gave him those years to fulfill his mission. Moses also had perfect eyesight and no loss of physical strength all the days of his life. (Deut. 34:4) The age of men declined gradually after the flood. The men of Israel who were twenty years old at the time of the Exodus died after forty years in the wilderness. None of them would have lived more than sixty years. However, Moses was a prophet, and he is describing life in general for the future generations.

"By one man (Adam) sin entered into the world, and death by sin; and death passed upon all men, for all have sinned." (Romans 5:12)

So teach us to number our days,
that we may apply our hearts to wisdom.
Return, O LORD, how long?
And let it repent thee concerning thy servants.
O satisfy us early with thy mercy;
that we may rejoice and be glad all our days.
Make us glad according to
the days wherein you have afflicted us,
and the years wherein we have seen evil. 90:12-15

We need God to teach us to know the brevity of our days on earth, so that we may have wisdom to prepare for eternity. Jesus said, "Lay up for yourselves treasures in heaven, where neither moth nor rust corrupt, and where thieves do not break through and steal. For where your treasure is, there will your heart be also." (Matt. 6:20-21) We suffer sicknesses and troubles, but they are God's way of teaching us that our earthly life is short and uncertain. "Therefore, we do not lose heart. Even though our outward man is perishing, yet the inward man is being renewed day by day. For our light affliction, which is but for a moment, is working for us a far more exceeding and eternal weight of glory, while we do not look at the things which are seen, but at the things which are not seen." NKJV (2 Corinthians 4:16-17)

Moses prays that the LORD will return with his mercy and forgive us when we sin. Israel had rebelled often, and God punished his nation. But the LORD does change his mind and his actions when men repent. (Jonah 3:10) Moses prays that we will be blessed with as many good days as we have suffered bad days.

> **Let your work be shown to your servants,**
> **and your glorious power to their children.**
> **And let the favor of the LORD our God be upon us,**
> **and establish the work of our hands upon us;**
> **yes, establish the work of our hands! 90:16-17** ESV

Moses prays that future generations would see how God cares for his faithful servants. God has shown his glorious power and grace. Although our earthly life is brief, the work that we have done for the LORD will be established by the good examples we have left for the next generation. "Blessed are the dead who die in the Lord. 'Yes,' says the Spirit, '… they may rest from their labors; and their works follow them.'" (Rev. 14:13)

Psalm 91

The Place of Safety

God is eternal, but man is frail. Only God can show us eternal salvation.

**He who dwells in the secret place of the Most High
  shall abide under the shadow of the Almighty.
I will say of the LORD,
  "He is my refuge and my fortress,
    my God, in him I will trust." 91:1-2**

Moses said in Psalm 90:1, God is "our dwelling place in all generations." The godly person sees God as his home, for he has a close relationship with the LORD. The believer will trust in God for his security and protection.

**Surely, he shall deliver you
  from the snare of the fowler, and
  from the deadly pestilence.
He shall cover you with his feathers,
  and under his wings you shall trust.
His trust shall be your shield and buckler. 91:3-4**

God will deliver the righteous from the snares of the ungodly and from deadly diseases. Even in death, God delivers the godly to be with him in Paradise. "Perfect love casts out fear." (1 John 4:18) God will protect his faithful children, as a hen protects her chicks under her wings. (Matthew 23:37) God is faithful as our shield.

**You shall not be afraid for the terror of night;
  nor for the arrow that flies by day;
  nor for the pestilence that walks in darkness;
  nor for the destruction that wastes at noonday.
A thousand shall fall at your side,
  and ten thousand at your right hand;
But it shall not come near you.
Only with your eyes shall you behold and see
  the reward of the wicked. 91:5-8**

Enemies may attack at night to kill, and armies usually fight in the daytime. A plague is personified as walking at night in search of victims and destroying others at noon. Though a thousand, even ten thousand, fall beside you in battle or by a plague, you will be protected. Jesus said, "Do not fear those who kill the body but cannot kill the soul." (Matt. 10:28) "He who overcomes shall inherit all things, and I will be his God and he shall be My son. But the cowardly, unbelieving, abominable, murderers, sexually immoral, sorcerers, idolaters, and all liars shall have their part in the lake which burns with fire and brimstone." NKJV (Rev. 21:7-8) Your eyes will see those who die without any hope beyond this earthly life.

> Because you have made the LORD, who is my refuge,
>   *even* the Most High, your habitation,
> There shall no evil befall you;
>   neither shall any plague come near your dwelling.
> For he shall give his angels charge over you,
>   to keep you in all your ways.
> They shall bear you up in their hands,
>   lest you dash your foot against a stone.
> You shall tread upon the lion and adder;
> The young lion and dragon you shall tread under feet.
>   **91:9-13**

Satan used verses 11-12 of this psalm to tempt Jesus. (Matthew 4:5-6) Jesus defeated Satan by quoting Deuteronomy 6:16, "You shall not tempt (test) the Lord your God." Time after time, the angels protected Jesus during his ministry when his enemies tried to kill him. But when the time came for him to be crucified, Jesus did not pray for protection, even though his Father could have provided more than twelve legions of angels to protect him. (Matthew 26:53) He knew it was God's will for him to die for our sins.

Angels are "ministering spirits sent forth to minister for those who will inherit salvation." ^{NKJV} (Hebrews 1:14) However, we are not to test God by putting ourselves in danger. We do not know how many times his angels have protected us from harm and sickness. But we should not think that God has abandoned us when it is God's will for us to suffer. The story of Job illustrates how God uses our sufferings to teach us important lessons. God's angels protected Paul (Acts 16:25-35), but God allowed him to suffer "a thorn in the flesh" sent by Satan to keep him humble. (2 Corinthians 12:7-19) God promises . . .

"Because he has set his love upon Me,
   therefore, I will deliver him.
I will set him on high,
   because he has known My name.
He shall call on Me, and I will answer him.
I will be with him in trouble;
I will deliver him, and honor him.
With long life, I will satisfy him,
And show him My salvation." 91:14-16 ^{NKJV}

These are the words of the LORD. God will deliver and honor those who love him with all their heart, soul, mind, and strength. (Mark 12:30) God will answer their prayers with his providential care. The godly life is the blessed life. Those who love and obey God will enjoy the blessings of an eternal home with him in heaven.

Psalm 92

Praise for God's Love and Faithfulness

A Song for the Sabbath Day

This psalm praises God for his love and faithfulness. He conquers our enemies, both personal and national. The song was for worship in the temple on the Sabbath.

> **It is a good thing to give thanks to the LORD,**
>   **and to sing praises to thy name, O Most High;**
> **To show forth your loving kindnesses in the morning,**
>   **and your faithfulness every night,**
> **Upon an instrument of ten strings, and**
> **Upon the psaltery,**
> **Upon on the harp with a solemn sound.**
> **For you, LORD, have made me glad through your work;**
> **I will triumph in the works of your hands. 92:1-4**

It is good to give thanks to God. Thanksgiving leads to happiness, contentment, and peace. That is why Paul and Silas were singing praises to God at midnight, although they had been beaten and placed in prison with their feet in stocks. (Acts 16:25) Singing praises to God lifts our spirit and encourages our soul. In the morning, we can thank God for the night's rest and pray for his strength and guidance to meet the challenges of the day. In the evening, we can thank him for the many blessings we have received during the day and seek his mercy and the forgiveness of our sins. We should praise him for his love and his faithfulness. His works will make us glad.

The psaltery was an ancient instrument called a lyre, which had ten strings; it resembled the zither. When Hezekiah restored the true worship in the temple, "he set the Levites … with cymbals, with psalteries, and with harps, according to the commandment of David, and Gad the king's seer, and Nathan the prophet: **for so was the commandment of the LORD.**" (2 Chronicles 29:25)   In the book of Psalms, God is to be praised with the use of man-made musical instruments. What a contrast to the New Testament! The new covenant of Christ does not command the use of mechanical musical instruments. We are to sing and make melody in our heart—not on the harp! (Ephesians 5:19) We are to use the instruments that God has made – our heart and vocal cords. If God wanted lyres and harps in Christian worship, he would have commanded their use as he did in the old covenant.

In the new covenant, there is not a separate priesthood to offer animal sacrifices, as commanded under the old covenant. (2 Chronicles 29:21) The law of Moses was "a shadow of good things to come, and not the very image of the things." (Hebrews 10:1) In fact, the Sabbath observance is not part of Christ's new covenant. "So let no one judge you in food, or in drink, or regarding a festival, or a new moon, or *sabbaths, which are a shadow of things to come; but the substance is of Christ."* NKJV (Colossians 2:16-17) Christ fulfilled the old covenant. We will triumph in the works of God!

> **O LORD, how great are your works!**
> **And your thoughts are very deep.**
> **A brutish man knows not,**
> **Neither does a fool understand this.**
> **When the wicked spring up as the grass,**
> **And when all the workers of iniquity flourish,**
> **It is that they shall be destroyed forever. 92:5-7**

God's creative and providential works are great. His thoughts and powers are beyond man's comprehension. We cannot explain how all things that are visible were made from invisible things. He spoke everything into existence. (Hebrews 11:3) We do not know how God answers prayers, but we do know he does. Isaiah asks,

"Who has understood the mind of the LORD, or instructed him as his counselor?" NIV (Isa. 40:13) "O the depth of the riches both of the wisdom and knowledge of God! How unsearchable are his judgments, and his ways past finding out!" (Romans 11:33)

Modern man thinks he knows more than the God of the Bible. The brutish person thinks that man is just an animal, and he denies the existence of God. "Professing themselves to be wise, they became fools." (Rom. 1:22) The ungodly spring up and grow like weeds. They seem to be invincible as they produce wickedness; but they shall be destroyed forever! (2 Peter 3:3-13)

> **But you, LORD, are most high forevermore.**
> **For, lo, your enemies, O LORD,**
> **For, lo, your enemies shall perish;**
> **All the workers of iniquity shall be scattered. 92:8-9**

The LORD is seated upon the highest throne. Heaven is his throne, and the earth is his footstool. (Isaiah 66:1) From everlasting to everlasting, he is God. (Psalm 90:1) All of his enemies will perish.

> **You have exalted my horn like that of a wild ox;**
> **fine oils have been poured out upon me.**
> **My eyes have seen the defeat of my adversaries;**
> **my ears have heard the rout of my wicked foes.**
> **92:10-11 NIV**

God gives us strength and power, which is symbolized by the horn of a wild beast. God's acceptance of us is symbolized by our being anointed with oil. (Psalm 23:5) God will punish our enemies even in our lifetime on earth. "For the wrath of God is revealed from heaven against all ungodliness and unrighteousness of men." (Romans 1:18) "For it is written, 'Vengeance is mine; I will repay, says the Lord.'" (Romans 12:19)

Psalm 94

The LORD Judges the Earth

O LORD God, to whom vengeance belongs—
O God, to whom vengeance belongs, shine forth!
Rise up, O Judge of the earth;
Render punishment to the proud.
LORD, how long will the wicked,
How long will the wicked triumph? 94:1-3 NKJV

We are not to take vengeance, because vengeance belongs to God. "It is written, 'Vengeance is mine; I will repay,' says the Lord." (Romans 12:19) This psalm calls upon the **Judge of the earth** to punish the proud who are prospering as they mistreat their fellowman.

How long shall they utter and speak hard things?
And all the workers of iniquity boast themselves?
They break in pieces your people, O LORD,
And afflict your heritage.
They slay the widow and the stranger,
And murder the fatherless.
Yet, they say, "The LORD shall not see,
Neither shall the God of Jacob regard it." 94:4-7

Wicked men sin with their boastful words. They also sin with their actions—they crush the faithful followers of God, and they destroy the widow, the fatherless and the stranger. They think God will not notice of them.

Understand, ye brutish among the people
   and ye fools.
When will ye be wise?
He who planted the ear, shall he not hear?
He who formed the eye, shall he not see?
He who chastises the heathen, shall not he correct?
He who teaches man knowledge, shall he not know?
The LORD knows the thoughts of man,
   that they are vanity. 94:8-11

The proud are acting like beasts without understanding. God, who made the ear, will hear their words. God, who made the eye, will see their actions. God, who punishes the nations, will punish them. God, who teaches man knowledge, knows all things. The LORD not only hears man's words and sees man's actions he even knows man's thoughts! (cf. Psalm 139)

> Blessed is the man whom you chasten, O LORD,
>   and teach him out of your law.
> That you may give him rest from the days of adversity,
>   until the pit is dug for the wicked.
> For the LORD will not cast off his people;
>   neither will he forsake his inheritance.
> But judgment shall return unto righteousness;
>   and all the upright in heart shall follow it. 94:12-15

The Hebrew word for **chasten** may also be translated **chastise, correct, instruct, teach**. When God chastens us, it "yields the peaceable fruit of righteousness," according to Hebrews 12:6-11. James wrote, "Consider it all joy, my brethren, when you encounter various trials, knowing that the testing of your faith produces endurance." (1:1-3) "You have heard of the endurance of Job and have seen the outcome of the Lord's dealings, that the Lord is full of compassion and is merciful." (5:11) NASB God instructs us through the adversities that we suffer. God allows Satan to afflict us to test our faith. Paul received "a thorn in the flesh, the messenger of Satan," to teach him that God's "grace is sufficient." God gives us strength to endure adversities. (2 Corinthians 12:7-10) Satan desires to harm us, but God provides the promises and the peace to overcome our trials. God will not forsake those who are upright in heart.

> Who will rise up for me against the evildoers?
> Who will stand up for me against the workers
>   of iniquity?

> Unless the LORD had been my help,
>   my soul had almost dwelt in silence.
> When I said, "My foot slips,"
>   your mercy, O LORD, held me up.
> In the multitude of my thoughts within me,
>   your comforts delight my soul. **94:16-19**

The psalmist says that he would have died without the LORD's help. He would have fallen, but the LORD held him up. God gives us both physical and spiritual strength. When going through trials, the thoughts of God bring us comfort, giving us hope and courage.

> Shall the throne of iniquity, which devises evil by law,
>   have fellowship with You?
> They gather together against the life of the righteous,
>   and condemn innocent blood.
> But the LORD has been my defense,
> And my God the rock of my refuge.
> He has brought on them their own iniquity,
> And shall cut them off in their own wickedness.
> The LORD our God shall cut them off. **93:20-23** NKJV

Wicked men may devise laws that condemn anyone who speaks against immoral acts. But they have no fellowship with God. Paul warns, "Do not be deceived, neither fornicators, nor idolaters, nor adulterers, nor homosexuals, nor sodomites, nor thieves, nor covetous, nor drunkards, nor revilers, nor extortioners will inherit the kingdom of God." And Paul later states, "The things which I write to you are the commandments of the Lord." NKJV (1 Cor. 6:9-10; 14:37) God is our defense.

God executes punishment upon the wicked even now. (Romans 1:18) This psalm describes the wickedness during the reign of Manasseh king of Judah. (2 Chron. 33:1-11) God is the Judge over the entire earth; he will cut off the wicked in their own wickedness. Vengeance belongs to God on the Day of Judgment! (Rom. 2:5-9)

Psalm 95

"Let Us Kneel before the LORD Our Maker"
Psalm 95:6

The Book of Hebrews quotes five verses of this psalm, and tells us that David is the writer. (Hebrews 4:7) After describing the LORD as our King in Psalm 93 and as our Judge in Psalm 94, this psalm refers to him as our Maker. Let us bow before our King, Judge and Maker!

> **O come, let us sing to the LORD;**
> **Let us make a joyful noise to the rock of our salvation.**
> **Let us come before his presence with thanksgiving,**
> **And make a joyful noise to him with psalms.**
> **For the LORD is a great King above all gods.**
> **In his hand are the deep places of the earth;**
> **The strength of the hills is his also,**
> **The sea is his, and he made it.**
> **And his hands formed the dry land. 95:1-5**

The LORD is to be praised with songs as our great King and as the Creator of the earth. Let us rejoice and give thanks to the One who has the power to save us.

> **O come, let us worship and bow down;**
> **Let us kneel before the LORD our Maker.**
> **For he is our God;**
> **And we are the people of his pasture,**
> **And the sheep of his hand. 95:6-7a**

Let us kneel before our God and worship him, because he created us. We belong to the LORD as sheep belong to the shepherd. Jesus said, "My sheep hear my voice, and I know them, and they follow me." (John 10:27)

> **Today, if you will hear His voice:**
> **"Do not harden your hearts, as in the rebellion,**
> **As in the day of trial in the wilderness,**
> **When your fathers tested Me;**
> **They tried Me, though they saw My work.**

For forty years I was grieved with that generation,
And said, 'It is a people who go astray in their hearts,
And they do not know My ways.'
So I swore in My wrath,
'They shall not enter My rest.'" 95:7b-11 ^{NKJV}

The LORD calls us by the Holy Scriptures to follow him. The New Testament says in Hebrews 3:7, "Therefore, as the Holy Spirit says, 'Today, if you will hear His voice, do not harden your hearts.'" The quotation is Psalm 95:7. The time to obey God is "today." Each day that we fail to obey God, the harder it becomes to live for him, and the easier it is to sin. Sheep obey the shepherd when they hear his voice.

We are warned not to harden our hearts as the people of Israel did in the wilderness. They accused Moses of bringing them out of Egypt to kill them with thirst. When God brought water from the rock, he called the place Massah, meaning "tested." (Exodus 17:7) They tested the patience of God. They had witnessed God's miraculous works, but they would not trust him to provide for them. They had gone **astray in their hearts**. They were not loving the LORD their God with all their heart. (Deut. 6:5) When they had the opportunity to enter their "rest" in the land of Canaan, they accused God, saying, "Why has the LORD brought us to this land to fall by the sword, that our wives and children should become victims?" (Num. 14:3) Because of their rebellion against the LORD, all who were twenty years of age and older died in the wilderness, except for Joshua and Caleb. (Numbers 14:29-30) After forty years, their children entered their land of "rest." God's leading Israel out of bondage in Egypt to their "rest" in Canaan foreshadowed our deliverance from the slavery of sin to our "rest" in heaven. "There remains therefore, a rest for the people of God." (Hebrews 4:9)

Psalm 96

"Sing to the LORD a New Song"

Oh, sing to the LORD a new song;
Sing to the LORD, all the earth.
Sing to the LORD, bless His name;
Proclaim the good news of His salvation
   from day to day.
Declare His glory among the nations,
His wonders among all peoples. 96:1-3 NKJV

The "new song" is a song of salvation. The redeemed from among men will sing "a new song" before God's throne in heaven, according to Revelation 14:1-5. We are to proclaim this good news among all nations today.

For the LORD is great, and greatly to be praised;
He is to be feared above all gods.
For all the gods of the nations are idols;
But the LORD made the heavens.
Honor and majesty are before him;
Strength and beauty are his sanctuary. 96:4-6

Reasons are given for our singing to the LORD a new song and praising his holy name. He is above all powers in heaven and on earth. He made the great universe. Such power is to be reverenced with godly fear. Heaven is his throne; the earth is his footstool. (Isaiah 66:1) He is surrounded by honor and majesty. He dwells in beauty and strength, for he is the source of all strength and the Creator of all beauty.

Give to the LORD, O families of the peoples,
Give to the LORD glory and strength.
Give to the LORD the glory due His name.
Bring an offering and come into His courts.
Oh, worship the LORD in the beauty of holiness!
Tremble before Him, all the earth. 96:7-9 NKJV

All the families of the earth are to praise the LORD for his glory and power. His name, representing his entire being, is glorious! **We are to worship the LORD in the beauty of holiness.** Jesus said, "true worshipers shall worship the Father in spirit and in truth; for the Father seeks such to worship him." (John 4:23) Our worship is beautiful and pleasing to God when it comes from our heart. Paul was speaking of his own spirit when he wrote, "I will pray with the spirit, and I will pray with the understanding also; I will sing with the spirit, and I will sing with the understanding also." (1 Cor. 14:15) Earlier, Paul asked the question, "Who knows a person's thoughts except the spirit of that person?" ESV (1 Cor. 2:11) We must be thinking about the glory and power and love of God as we worship him.

> **Say among the heathen that the LORD reigns.**
> **The world also shall be established**
>   **that it shall not be moved;**
> **He shall judge the people righteously.**
> **Let the heavens rejoice, and let the earth be glad;**
> **Let the sea roar, and the fulness thereof.**
> **Let the field be joyful, and all that is therein;**
> **Then shall all the trees of the wood rejoice**
>   **before the LORD.**
> **For he comes to judge the earth;**
> **He shall judge the world with righteousness,**
>   **and the people with his truth. 96:10-13**

The nations need to know about the LORD, for he reigns over the earth. He has established it, and it shall not be moved until the Day of Judgment. Because God is in control of nature, the heavens and earth may rejoice. He blesses the sea, the crops in the fields, and the trees in the forest. He is coming to judge the earth and the world with righteousness and truth. Romans 14:12 states, "So then every one of us shall give account of himself to God."

We can read of this judgment in 2 Peter 3:10-12, which says, "But the day of the Lord will come as a thief in the night, in which the heavens shall pass away with a great noise, and the elements shall melt with fervent heat; the earth also and the works that are therein shall be burned up. Seeing then that all these things shall be dissolved, what manner of persons ought ye to be in all holy conduct and godliness, looking for and hastening unto the coming of the day of God, wherein the heavens being on fire shall be dissolved, and the elements shall melt with fervent heat?"

Psalm 97

Rejoice in the LORD!

The LORD reigns, let the earth rejoice;
Let the many islands be glad.
Clouds and thick darkness surround Him;
Righteousness and justice are the foundation
    of His throne.
Fire goes before Him,
And burns up His adversaries round about.
His lightnings lit up the world;
The earth saw and trembled.
The mountains melted like wax at the presence of
    the LORD,
At the presence of the Lord of all the whole earth.
The heavens declare His righteousness,
And all the peoples have seen His glory. 97:1-6 NASB

The earth and all its peoples should rejoice, because the LORD reigns. As Isaac Watts said in his song of praise, "Let earth receive her King … And heaven and nature sing." When the LORD came down upon Mount Sinai, a thick cloud was on the mountain. This signified that God cannot be fully comprehended by man's limited under-standing. The foundation of the LORD's government is righteousness and justice. He descended upon the mount in fire. (Ex. 19:16-18) Fire represents judgment. When Jesus returns, he will be "revealed from heaven in blazing fire with his powerful angels. He will punish those who do not know God and do not obey the gospel of our Lord Jesus." ^{NIV} (2 Thessalonians 1:7-8) God's power is seen in his lightnings and in his thunders that shake the earth. When a volcanic mountain erupts, its lava fills the valleys like wax melting from a candle. The orderliness and beauty of the heavens proclaim God's righteousness and glory. "The heavens declare the glory of God; the skies proclaim the work of his hands." ^{NIV} (Psalm 19:1)

> **Let all those be ashamed who serve graven images,**
> **Who boast themselves of idols;**
> **Worship Him, all you gods.**
> **Zion heard this and was glad,**
> **And the daughters of Judah have rejoiced**
> **Because of Thy judgments, O LORD.**
> **For Thou art the LORD Most High over all the earth;**
> **Thou art exalted far above all gods. 97:7-9** ^{NASB}

When God judges idolatrous nations, he proves that their idols are powerless to save them. The "gods" here may refer to "supernatural powers," according to the notes in the New American Standard Bible. These are the powers Paul warns us about in Ephesians 6:12, "For we wrestle not against flesh and blood, but against principalities, against powers, against the rulers of the darkness of this age, against spiritual *hosts* of wickedness in the heavenly places." ^{NKJV} All these powers will submit to God's authority and judgments. Spiritual Zion and the righteous remnant of the Jews will rejoice.

> **Ye that love the LORD, hate evil.**
> **He preserves the souls of his saints;**
> **He delivers them out of the hand of the wicked.**

Light is sown for the righteous,
And gladness for the upright in heart.
Rejoice in the LORD, ye righteous;
And give thanks at the remembrance of his holiness.
                                              97:10-12

If we love the LORD, we will hate the evil; we will "abstain from every form of evil." ^{NKJV} (1 Thess. 5:22) Jesus said, "If you love Me, you will keep My commandments." ^{NASB} (John 14:15) The LORD will save those who are devoted to him. He gives light to the righteous. Paul instructs Christians to "rejoice in the Lord always" and "with thanksgiving let your requests be made known to God." (Philippians 4:4, 6)

Psalm 98

The LORD Has Done Marvelous Things

Oh, sing to the LORD a new song,
     for he has done marvelous things;
His right hand and his holy arm have
     gotten him the victory.
The LORD has made known his salvation;
His righteousness he has openly shown
     in the sight of the nations.
He has remembered his mercy and
     his truth to the house of Israel;
All the ends of the earth have seen the salvation
     of our God. 98:1-3

A new song was needed to praise the LORD for all the marvelous things he had done in the past. He created the heavens and the earth. He destroyed the wickedness upon the earth with a great world-wide flood in the days of Noah. All the nations knew how God saved the Israelites at the Red Sea from their slavery in Egypt. (Josh. 2:1-11) They saw God's power when David's army of Israel defeated all their enemies. His righteous wisdom was made known to the world by Solomon. When Israel seemed to be destroyed forever by the Assyrians and by the Babylonians, God remembered his mercy and his truth toward the nation of Israel, by returning them to their homeland to rebuild Jerusalem and the temple by the decree of Cyrus. (Ezra 1:1-4)

> **Shout for joy to the LORD, all the earth,**
> **burst into jubilant song and music;**
> **make music to the LORD with the harp,**
> **with the harp and the sound of singing,**
> **with trumpets and the blast of the ram's horn—**
> **shout for joy before the LORD, the King.**
> **98:4-6** NIV

After knowing about God's marvelous works, all the earth should joyfully praise the LORD, the ruling King.

> **Let the sea roar, and the fullness thereof;**
> **The world, and they that dwell therein.**
> **Let the floods clap their hands;**
> **Let the hills be joyful together before the LORD;**
> **For he comes to judge the earth;**
> **With righteousness he shall judge the world,**
> **and the people with equity. 98:7-9**

The roaring sea represented the ungodly powers of the world in Psalm 93:3-4, and the conquering Assyrians were represented by a flood in Isaiah 8:7-8. Now the sea and the floods rejoice at the coming of the LORD—the Messiah. The hills represent governments that would welcome him. (Isaiah 2:2-4) He would not only be their Savior he would also be their Judge. "For we must all appear before the judgment seat of Christ, that every one may receive the things done in the body, according to that he has done, whether good or bad." (2 Corinthians 5:10) Greater marvels are yet to come!

Psalm 99

The LORD Our God Is Holy

This is the last in the series of psalms that proclaim the LORD as King, beginning with Psalm 95.

> **The LORD reigns,**
> **let the nations tremble;**
> **he sits enthroned between the cherubim,**
> **let the earth shake.**
> **Great is the LORD in Zion,**
> **he is exalted over all the nations.**
> **Let them praise your great and awesome name—**
> **he is holy. 99:1-3** NIV

Everyone should reverence the LORD who is reigning! The temple's Most Holy Place represented the presence of the LORD. Two cherubim of gold faced each other with their wings overshadowing the mercy seat, the covering for the Ark of the Covenant. (Exodus 37:7-9)

When the LORD came down upon Mount Sinai, the earth **"quaked greatly"** and the people **"trembled."** (Exodus 19:16-18) The LORD is great in Zion, his dwelling place. His throne is heavenly Mount Zion. (Revelation 14:1-3) He is high above all the peoples of the earth. "Thus says the LORD, 'Heaven is My throne, and the earth is My footstool.'" (Isaiah 66:1) His entire being is awesome; he is to be praised for his divine attributes. He is totally pure and righteous—set apart from all other beings. His holiness is declared three times in this psalm. Yahweh our God, the eternal One, is holy!

> **The King is mighty, he loves justice—**
> **you have established equity;**
> **in Jacob you have done**
> **what is just and right.**
> **Exalt the LORD our God**
> **and worship at his footstool;**
> **he is holy. 99:4-5** NIV

The strength of the LORD our King is also seen in his love for justice; he judges without favoritism. In the history of the nation of Israel, his righteous judgments are demonstrated. The LORD our God is to be exalted and lifted up in praise and devotion. Solomon's temple in Jerusalem was "the footstool" of God. (1 Chron. 28:2-6; Lamentations 2:1) He rested his feet on the mercy seat in the Most Holy Place.

God's temple is now composed of Christians in Christ's church. (1 Cor. 3:16; Eph. 2:19-22; 1 Peter 2:5) We are exhorted, "And let us consider one another to provoke to love and to good works: not forsaking the assembling of ourselves together." (Hebrews 10:24-25) We are to exalt and worship the LORD our God because He is holy!

> **Moses and Aaron were among his priests;**
> **Samuel was among those who called on his name.**
> **They called on the LORD,**
> > **and he answered them.**
> **He spoke to them from the pillar of cloud;**
> > **they kept his statutes and the decrees**
> > > **he gave them.**
> **O LORD our God,**
> > **you answered them;**
> **you were to Israel a forgiving God,**
> > **though you punished their misdeeds.**
> **Exalt the LORD our God**
> > **and worship at his holy mountain,**
> > **for the LORD our God is holy. 99:6-9** NIV

God heard the prayers of Moses, Aaron, and Samuel, because they were seeking to do his will. Even though they came short of perfect obedience, God forgave them; but they suffered the consequences of their sins. Again, we are called to worship the LORD because He is holy. God's throne is on heavenly Mount Zion. (Rev. 14:1-3) Our desire should be to worship God in heaven.

Psalm 100

A Psalm of Thanksgiving

Make a joyful noise unto the LORD, all ye lands.
Serve the LORD with gladness;
    come before his presence with singing.
Know ye that the LORD he is God;
    it is **he that hath made us, and not we ourselves.**
We are his people, and the sheep of his pasture.
Enter into his gates with thanksgiving,
    and **into his courts with praise.**
Be thankful unto him, ***and*** **bless his name.**
For the LORD is good; his mercy is everlasting,
And his truth endures to all generations.

                                 100:1-5

All the inhabitants of the earth are to make a joyful noise (shout) to the LORD, the King of heaven and earth. A loud voice indicated earnestness of heart. When the nations of Ammon, Moab, and Edom came up against Judah during the reign of Jehoshaphat, the Levites stood up "to praise the LORD God of Israel with a loud voice." (2 Chronicles 20:19) We are to rejoice in the Lord always. (Ephesians 4:4)

In view of God's mercies, we should present our bodies as "a living sacrifice" to him; which is our "reasonable service." (Romans 12:1) Let's follow the example of Jesus, who said concerning the heavenly Father: "I always do those things that please Him." [NKJV] (John 8:29)

"Come before his presence with singing." This was a call to worship God in his temple at Jerusalem. The church is God's spiritual temple today. (1 Cor. 3:11-16) We must not forsake "the assembling of ourselves together" to worship God and to encourage each other to "love and good works." (Hebrews 10:24-25) We are to be "teaching and admonishing one another in psalms and hymns and spiritual songs, **singing** with grace in (our) hearts to the Lord." (Colossians 3:16)

"**Know ye that the LORD he is God.**" The name of the LORD is Yahweh, meaning self-existing and eternal. He is the only true God. Everyone needs to know the LORD as our Creator; we did not make ourselves through the process of evolution. We belong to him because he made us. He cares for us, as a shepherd cares for his sheep.

"**Enter into his gates with thanksgiving.**" We enter into our relationship with the LORD with thanksgiving for his many blessings. The apostle Paul writes, "Blessed be the God and Father of our Lord Jesus Christ, who has blessed us with all spiritual blessings in heavenly places in Christ, … in whom we have redemption through his blood, the forgiveness of sins, according to the riches of his grace." (Ephesians 1:3,7) "Every good gift … is from above and comes down from the Father." (James 1:17) The redeemed have an inheritance in heaven, that is incorruptible and does not fade away. (1 Peter 1:3-4)

"**And Bless his name.**" God's name stands for all his divine attributes. The LORD is to be praised for his infinite power, presence, knowledge, holiness, goodness, mercy, grace, faithfulness, truthfulness, justice, patience, his unchangeable nature and his love. His truth "endures to all generations." We should honor God, our benevolent King, who is merciful, truthful and eternal!

Psalm 101

Resolutions for Doing Right

A Psalm of David

This psalm may have been written when David was desiring to bring the Ark of the Covenant to Jerusalem, making it "the city of the LORD." (v. 8)

> **I will sing of mercy and justice.**
> **To You, O LORD, I will sing praises.**
> **I will behave wisely in a perfect way.**
> **Oh, when will You come to me?**
> **I will walk within my house with a perfect heart.**
> **101:1-2** NKJV

David makes resolutions for doing what is right. He praises God for his merciful love (*hesed*) and justice. The Hebrew word *hesed* describes love that is merciful, kind and steadfast; it is the Greek *agape* love that is described in 1 Corinthians 13. The word "justice" describes the right relationships among persons. [1]

David is seeking God's guidance. He promises to study and obey God's blameless way. He wants to bring the Ark of the Covenant to Jerusalem, because it represented the presence of God. He desires in his heart to be completely devoted to God and to his way. His "house" may refer both to his family and to his administration as the king of Israel.

> **I will set nothing wicked before my eyes.**
> **I hate the work of those who fall away;**
> **it shall not cling to me.**
> **A perverse heart shall depart from me;**
> **I will not know wickedness.**

---

[1] James Limburg, *Psalms,* p. 340

> Whoever secretly slanders his neighbor,
>> him I will destroy.
> The one who has a haughty look and a proud heart,
>> him I will not endure. **101:3-5** ^{NKJV}

David declares the things he will not tolerate. He will not look upon any worthless wicked thing. He will reject the work of apostates who depart from God's way. He will dismiss those from office who have an evil heart. David had suffered from slanderers during the reign of Saul; they would have no part in his reign. Slander and gossip spring from an arrogant heart.

> My eyes shall be upon the faithful of the land,
>> that they may dwell with me;
> He who walks in a blameless way is the one who
>> will minister to me. **101:6** ^{NASB}

David would surround himself with faithful followers of God. Those who would serve in his reign would be those who were above reproach.

> He who practices deceit shall not dwell within
>> my house;
> He who speaks falsehoods shall not maintain
>> his position before me.
> Every morning I will destroy all the wicked
>> of the land,
> So as to cut off from the city of the LORD,
>> all those who do iniquity. **101:7-8** ^{NASB}

Deceivers and liars would not be tolerated in Israel. David would constantly seek to rid Jerusalem of crime, for it is "the city of the LORD." These were David's resolutions for doing right. What are yours?

Psalm 102

A Prayer of Those in Exile

A Prayer of the afflicted, when he is overwhelmed,
and pours out his complaint before the LORD.

This is the prayer of the Jews while exiled in Babylon.
God had said that their captivity would last for seventy
years. (Jeremiah 29:10) Daniel could be the writer of this
psalm, because it is similar to his prayer in Daniel 9:1-19.
God's people were exhausted by oppression during the
reign of Belshazzar the king of Babylon. (Daniel 5)

> **Hear my prayer, O LORD,**
> **And let my cry come unto thee.**
> **Hide not thy face from me in the day**
> **when I am in trouble.**
> **Incline your ear unto me;**
> **in the day when I call, answer me speedily.**
> **For my days are consumed like smoke,**
> **and my bones are burned as a hearth.**
> **My heart is smitten,**
> **and withered like grass;**
> **So that I forget to eat my bread.**
> **By reason of the voice of my groaning**
> **my bones cleave to my skin,**
> **I am like a pelican of the wilderness;**
> **I am like an owl of the desert.**
> **I watch,**
> **And am as a sparrow alone upon the house top.**
> **102:1-7**

The psalmist is using figurative language to describe his
miserable condition. His days are passing like smoke into
nothingness. James 4:14 teaches us that our life "is even
a vapor, that appears for a little time, and then vanishes
away." His heart is like grass that is cut down and then
withers away. He is so depressed he forgets to eat.
Because of his sufferings, he feels like he is a living

skeleton, without fat and muscle. His loneliness is compared to the pelican and owl that inhabit deserted places and ruins. His sadness is compared to the sparrow.

> **My enemies reproach me all the day long;**
> **Those who deride me swear an oath against me.**
> **For I have eaten ashes like bread,**
> **And mingled my drink with weeping,**
> **Because of Your indignation and Your wrath;**
> **For You have lifted me up and cast me away.**
> **My days are like a shadow that lengthens,**
> **And I wither away like grass. 102:8-11** NKJV

The ridicule of enemies was added to the afflictions of the Jews in Babylon. They used the name of the Jews as a curse. It was a common form of cursing to wish a man the same fate as had come to one whose sufferings were well known. The ashes of humiliation had been their food. And their drink had been mixed with their tears. The LORD was punishing the Jews for their sins. God had lifted them up in the days of David and Solomon, but now he had cast them away. The nation of Israel was no more in their own homeland. The writer compares his days to the lengthening shadow on the sundial. He is growing older and withering away.

> **But thou, O LORD, shall endure forever,**
> **and thy remembrance unto all generations.**
> **You shall arise and have mercy upon Zion;**
> **for the time to favor her,**
> **Yes, the set time, is come.**
> **For thy servants take pleasure in her stones,**
> **and favor to the dust thereof.**
> **So, the heathen shall fear the name of the LORD,**
> **and all the kings of the earth thy glory.**
> **When the LORD shall build up Zion,**
> **he shall appear in his glory.**
> **He will regard the prayer of the destitute,**
> **and not despise their prayer.**

> **This will be written for the generation to come,**
> **and the people which shall be created**
> **shall praise the LORD.**
> **For he has looked down from the height of his**
> **sanctuary,**
> **From heaven the LORD did behold the earth,**
> **to hear the groaning of the prisoner,**
> **to release those that are appointed to death,**
> **to declare the name of the LORD in Zion,**
> **and his praise in Jerusalem,**
> **When the peoples are gathered together,**
> **And the kingdom, to serve the LORD. 102:12-22**

These words are written for the generation that was born in Babylonian exile and for generations to come. Although their present situation seemed to be hopeless, God would look down from his temple in heaven and see the sufferings of his people. He would deliver them from their captivity and rebuild his kingdom and his temple in Jerusalem, where they would worship him in Zion.

The temple was restored at Jerusalem. But the ultimate fulfillment of these verses was the creation of God's church/kingdom on the day of Pentecost in Jerusalem in Acts 2. God saw the suffering on earth due to those who were prisoners of sin. He sent Christ to deliver lost souls from spiritual death. The saved are gathered together in God's kingdom, and they are living stones in God's spiritual temple, the church. (Eph. 2:17-22)

After this earth has passed away, the saved will worship God before his throne in heavenly Zion. (Revelation 7:9-15; 14:1-3 and 21:1-7)

> **He weakened my strength in the way;**
> **He shortened my days.**
> **I said, "O my God, take me not away in the**
> **midst of my days;**
> **Thy years are throughout all generations.**

Of old thou hast laid the foundations of the earth;
And the heavens are the work of thy hands.
They shall perish, but you shall endure;
Yes, all of them shall wax old like a garment;
As a vesture you shall change them,
And they shall be changed.
But thou art the same,
And thy years shall have no end.
The children of thy servants shall continue,
And their seed shall be established before thee."

102:23-28

The writer returns to his own present condition. He is weak and his days are few. He prays that he might not die in the middle of man's normal life-span. In contrast with man's few days on earth, God has lived throughout all the generations of the children of men. The LORD created the earth and the heavens, which will perish. But God will continue forever. God's faithful servants, his new spiritual creation in Christ (v. 18), will endure forever with God in heaven. (Rev. 21:1-10, 24-27)

Verses 25-27 are quoted in Hebrews 1:10-12 and applied to Jesus Christ to prove his eternal nature and his divine power in the creation of all things. His physical life on earth was taken away in the middle of his years when he was offered as the atoning sacrifice for our sins; he was thirty-three years old. Jesus is our Savior indeed! He is God's gift of eternal love.

Psalm 103

Bless the LORD, O My Soul!

A Psalm of David

David first calls upon his own soul to "bless the LORD" in verses 1-5. Then he gives reasons why all who are in covenant relationship with God are to praise Him in verses 6-19. The angels of heaven are to "bless the LORD" in verses 20-22. And David concludes by saying again, "Bless the LORD, O my soul!" The word translated "bless" means more than to praise; "it is to praise with affection and gratitude." [2]

> **Bless the LORD, O my Soul!**
> **And all that is within me, bless his holy name.**
> **Bless the LORD, O my soul,**
> **And forget not all his benefits—**
> **Who forgives all your iniquities,**
> **Who heals all your diseases,**
> **Who redeems your life from destruction,**
> **Who crowns you with lovingkindness**
> **and tender mercies,**
> **Who satisfies your mouth with good things,**
> **So that your youth is renewed like the eagle's.**
> **103:1-5**

The LORD is to be praised with our entire being out of a heart of gratitude for all that he has done for us. God's benefits include the sufferings and hardships that have disciplined us to rely on Him—his healing our diseases, forgiving our sins, and saving us from eternal destruction. God had delivered David from death several times and had made him king of Israel. The LORD has shown us his steadfast love and mercies. He has given us forgiveness, strength and good things.

---

[2] G. Rawlinson, *The Pulpit Commentary, Vol. 6, Psalms*, p. 382

The LORD executes righteousness and judgment
    for all that are oppressed.
He made known his ways to Moses,
    his acts to the children of Israel.
The LORD is merciful and gracious,
    slow to anger and plenteous in mercy.
He will not always chide;
    neither will he keep his anger forever.
He has not dealt with us after our sins;
    nor rewarded us according to our iniquities.
For as the heaven is high above the earth,
    so great is his mercy toward them that fear Him.
As far as the east is from the west,
    so far has he removed our transgressions from us.
Like as a father pities his children,
    so the LORD pities them that fear him.
For he knows our frame;
    he remembers that we are dust.
As for man, his days are as grass;
    as a flower of the field, so he flourishes.
For the wind passes over it, and it is gone;
    and the place thereof shall know it no more.
But the mercy of the LORD is from everlasting
    to everlasting upon them who fear him,
    and his righteousness to children's children,
To such as keep his covenant,
    and to those who remember his commandments
    to do them.
The LORD has prepared his throne in heaven,
    and his kingdom rules over all. 103:6-19

The LORD will judge those who oppress his covenant people. He saved Israel from their oppression in Egypt, and he made his covenant with them on Mount Sinai. God revealed his way of righteousness to Moses and Israel. Whenever Israel forgot God and worshiped idols, God punished them with oppressors. But when the people repented, he removed their sins far from them. God did not keep his anger forever because he is merciful and gracious. James Limburg explains what this means: "The Hebrew root for the word translated 'merciful' is *rehem,* 'womb.' Thus the picture behind 'merciful' is the kind of affection a mother has for a child of her own womb; the word could be translated 'motherly love.'" [3]

God also deals with his people as a Father understands and feels for his children. He knows our weakness and frailty. He gives mercy to those who reverence him and seek to obey his will. The LORD is involved in our lives on earth as he rules over his kingdom from his throne in heaven. "And we know that God causes all things to work together for good to those who love God, to those who are called according to his purpose." [NASB] (Romans 8:28)

> **Bless the LORD, ye his angels,**
> **who excel in strength, that do his commandments,**
> **hearkening to the voice of his word.**
> **Bless ye the LORD, all ye his hosts,**
> **ye ministers of his, that do his pleasure.**
> **Bless the LORD, all his works in all places of his**
> **dominion.**
> **Bless the LORD, O my soul. 103:20-23**

I am to join with the angels of heaven and the entire creation of the universe in heart-felt praise to the Eternal God, the Great I AM!

This psalm would have been a comfort to the Jews who were suffering while in Babylon as described in the previous psalm. Regardless of how hopeless our lives may seem to be, we can be assured of God's love for us by David's words in Psalm 103.

---

[3] James Limburg, *Psalms,* p. 149

Psalm 104

How Great Thou Art!

Like Psalm 103, this psalm begins and ends with, "Bless the LORD, O my soul." In Psalm 103, David praises God for his steadfast love and compassion. In Psalm 104, he praises the LORD for his great creative works and sustaining power.

Bless the LORD, O my soul!

O LORD my God, thou art very great!
Thou art clothed with honor and majesty,
Who covers thyself with light as with a garment,
Who stretches out the heavens like a curtain.
Who lays the beams of his chambers in the waters,
Who makes the clouds His chariot,
Who walks on the wings of the wind,
Who makes His angels spirits,
     his ministers a flaming fire. 104:1-4

"God is light." (1 John 1:5) Light reveals things as they truly are; light reveals the truth. "God said, 'Let there be light,' and there was light." (Gen. 1:3) Jesus Christ said, "I am the light of the world; he who follows me shall not walk in darkness, but shall have the light of life." (John 8:12) "The glory of God" illuminates his heavenly city. (Rev. 21:23) The beautiful skies during both the day and night cover the earth like a tent.

God separated the water in the sky from the water on earth on the second day of creation. (Gen. 1:6-8) God's dwelling place is high above the clouds.

Verse four is quoted in Hebrews 1:7 to describe the work of angels. They are swift in carrying out God's orders and judgments.

He set the earth on its foundations,
so that it should never be moved. 104:5 ESV

God "hangs the earth upon nothing." (Job 26:7) Yet, it is firmly established upon its invisible foundations. Its rotation upon its axis is so precise that we can always measure a twenty-four-hour day. The earth's orbit around the sun remains the same. We can measure a year with accuracy. The slight tilt of the earth on its axis gives us our predictable summers and winters.

You covered it with the deep as with a garment;
the waters stood above the mountains.
At thy rebuke they fled;
at the voice of thy thunder, they hasted away.
They go up by the mountains;
They go down by the valleys unto the place
which you have established for them.
You have set a boundary that they may not pass over;
that they turn not again to cover the earth.
104:6-9

Water covered the entire earth like a garment when it was created in the beginning. (Genesis 1:1-2) But on the third day of creation, God said, "Let the waters under the heaven be gathered to gather unto one place, and let the dry land appear." (Gen. 1:9-13) **The mountains rose; the valleys sank down** providing a place for the waters to be gathered.

During the days of Noah, a flood covered the entire earth again with waters rising above the mountains. But after the flood, God set a rainbow in the cloud to be a sign of his covenant that the waters shall not cover the entire earth again. (Gen. 9:11-17)

He sends the springs into the valleys;
They flow among the hills.
They give drink to every beast of the field;
The wild donkeys quench their thirst.
By them the birds of the heavens have their home;
They sing among the branches.
He waters the hills from His upper chambers;
The earth is satisfied with the fruit of Your works.
104:10-13 ^{NKJV}

Springs of water flow into ravines and become creeks
and rivers that provide water for all the animals and birds.

He makes grass to grow for the cattle,
and plants for man to cultivate—
bringing forth food from the earth:
wine that gladdens the heart of man,
oil to make his face shine,
and bread that sustains his heart.
The trees of the LORD are well watered,
the cedars of Lebanon that he planted.
There the birds make their nests;
the stork has its home in the pine trees.
The high mountains belong to the wild goats;
the crags are a refuge for the coneys. 104:14-18 ^{NIV}

God made vegetables for man and grass for the animals.
God "gave us rain from heaven and fruitful seasons,
filling our hearts with food and gladness." (Acts 14:17)
God created a suitable place for man to live, and he made
various habitats for all kinds of animals and birds.

He made the moon to mark the seasons;
the sun knows its time for setting.
You make darkness, and it is night,
when all the beasts of the forest creep about.
The young lions roar after their prey,
seeking their food from God.
When the sun rises, they steal away
and lie down in their dens.

> **Man goes out to his work**
> **and to his labor until the evening. 104:19-23** ᴱˢⱽ

Our time is divided into months due to the completion of the moon' orbit around our earth. The Jews observed the first day of the lunar month as a holy day. (Numbers 28:11-15) God's creation gives us day and night. "And God said, 'Let there be lights in the expanse of the sky to separate the day from the night, and let them serve as signs to mark seasons and days and years, and let them be lights in the expanse of the sky to give light on the earth.' And it was so. God made two great lights—the greater light to govern the day and the lesser light to govern the night. He also made the stars." ᴺᴵⱽ (Gen. 1:14-16) At night, the wild animals go out in search of their prey, and they rest during the day. Man works during the daytime hours and sleeps at night.

> **O LORD, how manifold are thy works!**
> **In wisdom thou hast made them all;**
> **The earth is full of thy riches.**
> **So is this great and wide sea,**
> **wherein are things creeping innumerable,**
> **both small and great beasts.**
> **There go the ships;**
> **there is that Leviathan, whom thou hast made**
> **to play therein. 104:24-26**

God's wisdom and power are seen in the things he has made. (Romans 1:19-20) The earth is rich in precious metals. Soil contains minerals that plants, animals and man need. Wood, coal, oil and electricity provide heat and energy to bless us. The great oceans and seas provide the water cycle that gives life to all living things. God has designed all kinds of insects, fish, birds, animals and man. God created man with intelligence to make ships to sail on the seas and airplanes to fly in the air. Everything God has made has a purpose.

> These all look to you to give them food
>> at the proper time.
> When you give it to them, they gather it up;
> When you open your hand, they are satisfied
>> with good things.
> When you hide your face, they are terrified;
> When you take away their breath, they die
>> and return to the dust.
> When you send your Spirit, they are created,
>> and you renew the face of the earth.
>> **104:27-30** NIV

God provides food and nourishment for all of his living creation. That is why we should pray, "Give us this day our daily bread." (Matt. 6:11) During famine and other natural disasters, food may become scarce, and we are reminded of our dependence upon God. All living things, including man, die and return to the dust. But God put seed in his creation of grass, herb, tree, fish, bird, animal and man. (Genesis 1:11, 22, 28) So, the earth is renewed by God who gives life to the next generation.

> Let the glory of the LORD endure forever;
> Let the LORD be glad in His works;
> He looks on the earth, and it trembles;
> He touches the mountains, and they smoke.
> I will sing to the LORD as long as I live;
> I will sing praise to my God while I have my being.
> Let my meditation be pleasing to Him;
> As for me, I shall be glad in the LORD.
> Let the sinners be consumed from the earth,
> And let the wicked be no more. 104:31-35 NASB

God's glory will last forever. He rejoices in the earth, but he judges it with his power. He was not pleased with his creation; so, he sent a great flood upon the entire earth which destroyed all mankind and the animals and the birds except for those in Noah's ark. (Genesis 6:5-7)

The earth is said to tremble (an anthropomorphism) when God sees the wickedness that is now in the world. "But the present heavens and earth by His word are being reserved for fire, kept for the day of judgment and destruction of ungodly men." NASB (2 Peter 3:7) When the LORD came down on Mount Sinai to give his Law to Israel, smoke covered the mountain, and it quaked greatly. (Exodus 19:18)

As the psalmist rejoices in the LORD, he prays that his meditation will be pleasing to him. Man is blessed when he meditates on God's word and his works. (Psalm 1:2) God wants us to delight in him, because he knows what is best for us.

The fourth petition is for sinners not to be in the earth. Sin has been the cause of man's troubles and sorrows. The psalmist prays for the wicked to be no more. Our present heavens and earth will be destroyed. "We, according to his promise, look for new heavens and a new earth wherein dwells righteousness." (2 Peter 3:10-13) In the holy new Jerusalem, "nothing impure will ever enter it, nor will anyone who does what is shameful or deceitful." NIV (Revelation 21:1-3, 27) The throne of God shall be in it. (Revelation 22:3)

> **Bless the LORD, O my soul!**
> **Praise ye the LORD. 104:35**

Again, the psalmist tells his soul to praise the LORD. He encourages everyone to join him in the praise saying, **"Hallelujah!"** This praise is repeated in Revelation 19:1, "Hallelujah! Salvation and glory and power belong to our God, for true and just are his judgments." NIV

Psalm 105

God Remembers His Covenant

This psalm praises God for remembering his covenant
with Abraham, Isaac and Jacob. He promised to make of
them a great nation. (Genesis 12:1-3; 26:1-4; 28:13-14)
David wrote the first fifteen verses of Psalm 105 to thank
the LORD when the ark of the covenant was set inside the
tabernacle in Jerusalem. (1 Chronicles 16:1, 7, 8-22)

> **O give thanks to the LORD!**
> **Call upon his name;**
> **Make known his deeds among the people!**
> **Sing to him, sing psalms to him;**
> **Talk of all his wondrous works!**
> **Glory in his holy name;**
> **Let the heart of them rejoice who seek the LORD!**
> **Seek the LORD and his strength;**
> **Seek his face evermore!**
> **Remember his marvelous works that he has done,**
> **His wonders and the judgments of his mouth,**
> **O ye seed of Abraham his servant,**
> **Ye children of Jacob, his chosen! 105:1-6**

Those who are the **seed of Abraham** are to give thanks
to the LORD. This includes Christians. "For ye are all the
children of God by faith in Christ Jesus. For as many of
you as have been baptized into Christ have put on Christ.
… **And if you are Christ's, then you are Abraham's
seed, and heirs according to the promise.**" (Galatians
3:26-29) We are to tell others about God's wonderful
works. We are to "call upon his name" in prayer for
strength and wisdom. (James 1:5) This often was the
prayer of David. We are to rejoice and seek the Lord
through his revealed word. (Deuteronomy 29:29; John
6:63; 2 Timothy 2:15; 2 Peter 1:3-8) Let's remember
God's marvelous works and judgments.

He is the LORD our God;
    his judgments are in all the earth.
He has remembered his covenant forever,
    the word *which* he commanded
    to a thousand generations.
Which *covenant* he made with Abraham,
`   and his oath to Isaac,
And confirmed the same to Jacob for a law,
    and to Israel *for* an everlasting covenant:
Saying, "Unto you I will give the land of Canaan,
    the lot of your inheritance,"
When they were *but* a few men in number,
    yes, very few, and strangers in it. 105:7-12

The great I AM is our God. His judgments upon man's ungodliness can be seen throughout the earth. (Romans 1:18-32) However, He remembers his covenant with his people forever. He promised the land of Canaan to Abraham, Isaac and Jacob when they were few and strangers in that land. As he kept his promises to Israel, God will keep his new covenant with spiritual Israel. (Galatians 6:15-16) Although faithful Christians may be few in number, God has promised that they will receive heaven as an inheritance. (John 14:1-6 and Rev. 21:4-7)

When they went from one nation to another,
From one kingdom to another people,
He suffered no man to do them wrong;
Yes, he reproved kings for their sakes,
Saying, "Touch not my anointed,
And do my prophets no harm." 105:13-15

At God's promise, Abraham left the city of Ur in Chaldea and went to the land of Canaan, where there were several nations. During a famine, Abraham went to Egypt and later returned to the people of Canaan. God reproved a Pharaoh in Egypt and later a Philistine king. (Genesis 12:1-20; 20:1-18; Acts 7:2-4)

And He called for a famine upon the land;
He broke the whole staff of bread.
He sent a man before them,
Joseph, who was sold as a slave.
They afflicted his feet with fetters;
He himself was laid in irons,
Until the time that his word came to pass,
The word of the LORD tested him.
The king sent and released him,
The ruler of peoples, and set him free.
He made him lord of his house,
And ruler over all his possessions,
To imprison his princes at will,
That he might teach his elders wisdom.

105:16-22 ^{NASB}

God can control the weather! God can call for a famine upon the land! Before he sent the famine, he sent Joseph as a slave to Egypt. We can see the providence of God working in the life of Joseph.

In dreams, God told Joseph that he would be a ruler; and this caused his brothers to envy and hate him. When he was seventeen, they sold him to be a slave in Egypt. (Genesis 37) Joseph served Potipher so well that he was made the overseer of his master's house, and the LORD blessed him. When Potiphar's wife falsely accused Joseph, he was thrown into prison. (Genesis 39) While in prison, Joseph interpreted correctly the dreams of the king's butler and baker. The butler was released from prison to serve the king, and the baker was hanged. (Genesis 40)

Two years later, Pharaoh had dreams that troubled him, and the butler told him about Joseph's ability to interpret dreams. Joseph told the king that there would be seven years of great plenty followed by seven years of famine throughout the land. Pharaoh set Joseph "over all the land of Egypt" to gather up grain during the seven years of plenty so there would be food during the seven years of famine. "So all countries came to Joseph in Egypt to buy grain, because the famine was severe in all lands." ᴺᴷᴶⱽ (Genesis 41) Years later, Joseph told his brothers who had sold him as a slave, "You meant evil against me, but God meant it for good, in order to bring it about as it is this day, to save many people alive." ᴺᴷᴶⱽ (Genesis 50:20)

> **Israel also came into Egypt,**
>> **and Jacob sojourned in the land of Ham.**
> **And he increased his people greatly,**
>> **and made them stronger than their enemies.**
> **He turned their heart to hate his people,**
>> **to deal craftily with his servants. 105:23-25**

God had given Jacob the name **Israel**, which means "power with God." (Genesis 32:27-28) The LORD was with Jacob when he went to live in Egypt because of the famine. Jacob's descendants multiplied greatly. God blessed the people of Israel and made them strong. This caused the Egyptians to fear the Israelites. So, they made them their slaves. (Exodus 1:7-13)

> **He sent Moses His servant,**
> *And* **Aaron whom He had chosen.**
> **They showed His signs among them,**
> **And wonders in the land of Ham. 105:26-27**

Moses and Aaron were sent to perform ten plagues on the Egyptians, descendants of Ham. (Genesis 10:1-6,13)

> **He sent darkness, and made it dark;**
> **And they did not rebel against His word.**
> **He turned their waters into blood, and killed their fish.**
> **Their land abounded with frogs,**
> *Even* **in the chambers of their kings.**
> **He spoke, and there came swarms of flies,**
> *And* **lice in all their territory.**

> He gave them hail for rain,
> And flaming fire in their land.
> He struck their vines also, and their fig trees,
> And splintered the trees of their territory.
> He spoke, and locusts came,
> Young locusts without number,
> And ate up all the vegetation in their land.
> And devoured the fruit of their ground.
> He also destroyed all the firstborn in their land,
> The first of all their strength. 105:28-36 NKJV

God showed his great power over the Egyptians. God still uses natural disasters to cause people to repent. But the majority are like Pharaoh, who did not truly repent. (Rev. 8:7-21) Moses and Aaron obeyed God's word, and led Israel out of their slavery after the tenth plague, the death of the firstborn in Egypt. (Exodus 7:14 – 11:10)

> He brought out Israel, laden with silver and gold,
>   and from among their tribes no one faltered.
> Egypt was glad when they left,
>   because dread of Israel had fallen on them.
> He spread out a cloud as a covering,
>   and a fire to give light at night.
> They asked, and he brought them quail
>   and satisfied them with the bread of heaven.
> He opened the rock, and water gushed out;
>   like a river it flowed in the desert. 105:37-41 NIV

When the Israelites asked for clothing and articles of silver and gold, the Egyptians granted their requests because they feared the God of Israel. (Exodus 12:30-36) God gave the Israelites strength to leave Egypt, and he guided them with "a pillar of cloud" by day and "a pillar of fire" by night. (Exodus 13:21-22) The cloud covered and protected them from the hot desert sun by day, and the fire overhead gave them sufficient light at night. He fed them with quail and with "the bread of heaven,"

which they called Manna. (Exodus 16:11-31) On two
occasions, the LORD gave them water from a rock to drink
when they were thirsty. (Exodus 17 and Numbers 20)

> **For He remembered his holy promise,**
>> ***and* Abraham his servant.**
> **And He brought forth his people with joy,**
>> ***and* his chosen with gladness.**
> **And He gave them the lands of the heathen,**
>> **and they inherited the labor of the people,**
> **That they might observe his statues,**
>> **and keep his laws.**
> **Praise the LORD! 105:42-45**

The LORD remembered his promise to Abraham that he
would make him into a great nation, and all the families
of the earth would be blessed. (Genesis 12:1-3) God gave
the descendants of Abraham the land of Canaan, and they
entered it with great joy! God kept his covenant! He gave
the Israelites these special blessings so that they would be
an example to the world by obeying his commandments.

The promise to Abraham is explained by the apostle
Paul, ***"It is those who are of faith that are the sons of
Abraham. And the Scripture, foreseeing that God would
justify the Gentiles by faith, preached the gospel before-
hand to Abraham, saying, 'All the nations shall be
blessed in you.' So then those who are of faith are
blessed with Abraham, the believer."*** NASB (Gal. 3:7-9)

The following words were written to Christians: "You
are a chosen generation, a royal priesthood, a holy nation,
His own special people, that you may proclaim the praises
of Him who called you out of darkness into His marvelous
light ... Beloved, I beg you as sojourners and pilgrims,
abstain from fleshly lusts which war against the soul,
having your conduct honorable among the Gentiles." NKJV
(2 Peter 2:9, 11)   Praise the LORD!

Psalm 106

Praise the LORD

This psalm was likely written after the Jews returned from their exile in Babylon. (vv. 46-47) They were restoring the worship of God in Jerusalem. (Ezra 1:1-4) The psalm begins and ends with "Praise the LORD!"

> **Praise the LORD!**
> **Oh, give thanks to the LORD, for He is good;**
> **For His lovingkindness is everlasting.**
> **Who can speak of the mighty deeds of the LORD,**
> **Or can show forth all His praise?**
> **How blessed are those who keep justice,**
> **Who practice righteousness at all times! 106:1-3** NASB

We are to thank the LORD because He alone is totally good. (Mark 10:18) We are to thank him for his love and mercy. No one knows all the mighty deeds of God. No one is able to give all the praises that are due to him. We are blessed when we do what is right. In obeying God, "there is great reward." (Psalm 19:9-11)

> **Remember me, O LORD,**
> **in *Thy* favor toward Thy people;**
> **Visit me with Thy salvation,**
> **That I may see the prosperity of Thy chosen ones,**
> **That I may rejoice in the gladness of Thy nation,**
> **That I may glory with Thine inheritance. 106:4-5** NASB

Christians are now God's "holy nation, His own special people." (2 Peter 2:9-10) We may be going through difficult times because of our own sins or the sins of others. But God remembers his own people. Jesus said to his disciples, ***"In the world, you will have tribulation; but be of good cheer. I have overcome the world."*** NKJV (John 16:13) God will deliver us from the trials of this world and give us an inheritance with Him in heaven.

We have sinned with our fathers,
We have committed iniquity,
We have done wickedly. 106:6

Daniel understood the writings of the prophet Jeremiah that the seventy years of exile in Babylon would soon be over; and he wrote, *"We have sinned and committed iniquity and have done wickedly."* **(Daniel 9:5)** We are to repent and confess our sins. (Read Jeremiah 29:10-14.)

Our fathers understood not thy wonders in Egypt;
They remembered not the multitude of thy mercies,
But provoked him at the sea, even at the Red Sea.
106:7

Their fathers provoked the LORD at the Red Sea by saying, "Have you taken us away to die in the wilderness? Why have you dealt with us, to bring us up out of Egypt? Is this not the word that we told you in Egypt, saying, 'Let us alone that we may serve the Egyptians?' For it would have been better for us to serve the Egyptians than to die in the wilderness." NKJV (Ex. 14:11-12) The Israelites forgot God's power.

Earlier when Moses and Aaron spoke to the elders of Israel and showed them the "signs" of the LORD proving God's power to deliver them from their slavery, the people believed. (Exodus 4:29-31) But they thought their deliverance would come soon without any suffering. After Moses and Aaron spoke to Pharaoh, he increased his afflictions upon the Israelites; and they complained to Moses, saying, "You have made us abhorrent in the sight of Pharaoh and in the sight of his servants, to put a sword in their hand to kill us." NKJV (Exodus 4:20-21)

The LORD delayed his deliverance of Israel in order to show his power. When God brought the ten plagues upon the Egyptians, the Israelites did not understand God's wonders and his purpose in sending the plagues, and they forgot his mercies in sparing them from most of plagues. (Exodus 8:22)

When hardships come to us, God has a purpose. James tells us, "Consider it all joy, my brethren, when you encounter various trials, knowing that the testing of your faith produces endurance. And let endurance have its perfect result, that you may be perfect and complete, lacking in nothing. But if anyone of you lacks wisdom, let him ask of God, who gives to all men generously and without reproach, and it will be given to him. But let him ask in faith without any doubting, for the one who doubts is like the surf of the sea driven and tossed by the wind. For let not that man expect that he will receive anything from the Lord." NASB (James 1:2-7)

Let's get God's viewpoint. It's easy to be nearsighted when trials come. Peter writes, "For this very reason, make every effort to add to your faith goodness; and to goodness, knowledge; and to knowledge, self-control; and to self-control, perseverance; and to perseverance, godliness; and to godliness, brotherly kindness; and to brotherly kindness, love. For if you possess these qualities in increasing measure, they will keep you from being ineffective and unproductive in your knowledge of our Lord Jesus Christ. But if anyone does not have them, he is nearsighted and blind." NIV (2 Peter 1:5-9)

> Nevertheless, he saved them for his name's sake,
>   that he might make his mighty power to be known.
> He rebuked the Red Sea also, and it was dried up;
>   so, he led them through the depths,
>   as through the wilderness.
> And he saved them from the hand of him
>   that hated them,
> And redeemed them from the hand of the enemy.
> And the waters covered their enemies;
> There was not one of them left.

Then they believed his words;
They sang his praise. 106:8-12

Moses spoke to the Israelites at the Red Sea, saying to them, "Fear not, stand still, and see the salvation of the LORD." (Exodus 14:13) God showed his great power by dividing the waters and drying up a path in the sea through which he led them. Their enemy, the Egyptian army, was destroyed by the waters of the sea. (Exodus 14:27-28) Then Moses and the children of Israel praised God in song. (Exodus 15:1- 19) The name of the LORD and his power over at the Red Sea was still known by the Canaanites in Jericho forty years later. (Joshua 2:1-10)

They soon forgot His works;
They did not wait for His counsel,
But lusted exceedingly in the wilderness,
And tested God in the desert.
And He gave them their request,
But sent leanness into their soul. 106:13-15 NKJV

Their faith was short-lived. Only three days later in the wilderness at Marah, the waters were bitter. Instead of praying for God's help, "the people murmured against Moses, saying, 'What shall we drink?'" (Ex. 15:22-24)

On the fifteenth day of the second month after departing from Egypt, they again showed their lack of faith in God to provide for them. They accused Moses and Aaron of bringing them into the wilderness "to kill" them "with hunger." (Exodus 16:1-3) Moses told the people, "Your murmurings are not against us, but against the LORD." (Exodus 16:8) God provided bread for them to eat, manna. (Exodus 16:14-15) Later, Jesus would say, "I am the Bread of Life." (John 6:32-35)

Later, the people complained, "Who will give us meat to eat. We remember the fish which we ate freely in Egypt, the cucumbers, the melons, the leeks, the onions and the garlic; but now … there is nothing at all except this manna before our eyes." ᴺᴷᴶⱽ (Numbers 11:4-6) So, the LORD sent a large number of quail. While they were feasting on the meat, "the LORD struck the people with a very great plague." ᴺᴷᴶⱽ (Numbers 11:31-33)

> **They envied Moses also in the camp,**
> ***And* Aaron the saint of the LORD.**
> **The earth opened and swallowed Dathan,**
> **And covered the company of Abiram.**
> **And a fire was kindled in their company;**
> **And the flame burned up the wicked. 106:16-18**

Korah, Dathan and Abiram led the Levites in a rebellion against Moses and Aaron. This story is Numbers 16. The earth opened and swallowed Dathan and Abiram. Fire from the LORD consumed Korah.

> **They made a calf in Horeb,**
> **and worshiped a metal image.**
> **They exchanged the glory of God**
> **for the image of an ox that eats grass.**
> **They forgot God, their Savior,**
> **who had done great things in Egypt,**
> **wondrous works in the land of Ham,**
> **and awesome deeds by the Red Sea.**
> **Therefore he said he would destroy them—**
> **had not Moses, his chosen one,**
> **stood in the breach before him,**
> **to turn away his wrath from destroying them. ᴱˢⱽ**
> **106:19-23**

This story takes place at Mount Sinai, where God had spoken the ten commandments to his people just a week or two earlier. Because Moses delayed coming down from the mountain, the people thought something had happened to him. So, they asked Aaron to make gods for them. They forgot God, their Savior, who had delivered them at the Red Sea from their slavery to the Egyptians.

They began worshiping a golden metal lifeless calf that they had made. (Ex. 32) Again, we see their impatience. Let's learn not to make this same mistake. When things don't go our way, we are tempted to forget God. The LORD would have destroyed the nation of Israel and made of Moses his nation. But Moses earnestly interceded for the Israelites. Let's not forget our Savior!

> **Then they despised the pleasant land;**
> **they did not believe his promise.**
> **They grumbled in their tents**
> **and did not obey the LORD.**
> **So he swore to them with uplifted hand**
> **that he would make them fall in the desert,**
> **make their descendants fall among the nations**
> **and scatter them throughout the lands.** NIV
> **106:24-27**

The refusal of Israel to enter the land that God had promised to give them is recorded in Numbers 13-14. The majority of those who spied out the land of Canaan told the Israelites, "We are not able to go up against the people, for they are stronger than we. There we saw the giants; and we were like grasshoppers in our own sight, and so we were in their sight." (Num. 13:31,33) The whole congregation of Israel wept that night. In the morning, they said to Moses and Aaron, "Why has the LORD brought us to this land to fall by the sword?" They did not believe God had the power to give them the land of Canaan as he had promised them. They wanted to return to Egypt. (Numbers 14:1-4)

Joshua and Caleb encouraged them to obey God, saying, "If the LORD delight in us, then he will bring us into this land, and give it to us; a land which flows with milk and honey. Only rebel not against the LORD." But all the congregation was ready to stone them with stones when the glory of the LORD appeared. (Numbers 14:6-10)

The LORD said, "Because all these men who have seen My glory and the signs which I did in Egypt and in the wilderness, and have put Me to the test now these ten times, and have not heeded My voice; they certainly shall not see the land which I swore to the fathers." (14:22-23) "The carcasses of you who have complained against Me shall fall in this wilderness, ... from twenty years old and above. Except for Caleb and Joshua, you shall by no means enter the land. But your little ones, I will bring them in, and they shall know the land which you have despised." ^{NKJV} (14:29-31) In the future, their descendants would be scattered among the nations for similar sins.

> **They yoked themselves to the Baal of Peor**
>> **and ate sacrifices offered to lifeless gods;**
> **they provoked the LORD to anger**
>> **by their wicked deeds,**
>> **and a plague broke out among them.**
> **But Phinehas stood up and intervened,**
>> **and the plague was checked.**
> **This was credited to him as righteousness**
>> **for endless generations to come. 106:28-31** ^{NIV}

After forty years in the wilderness, the nation of Israel camped in the plains of Moab in preparation to enter the land of Canaan. This story is in Numbers 25. "The men began to indulge in sexual immorality with Moabite women, who invited them to the sacrifices to their gods. So Israel joined in worshiping the Baal of Peor. And the LORD's anger burned against them." (vv. 1-3) God sent a plague among the camp of Israel, and 24,000 died. (v. 9) Phinehas, the young son of Eleazar the high priest, followed the LORD's command by driving a spear through an Israelite man and into a Midian woman's body as they sinned. Then the plague stopped. The LORD made a covenant with Phinehas stating that his descendants would have a lasting priesthood. (v. 13)

> **They angered Him also at the waters of strife,**
> **So that it went ill with Moses for their sakes;**
> **Because they provoked his spirit,**
> **So that he spoke unadvisedly with his lips. 106:32-33**

This story is in Numbers 20. It occurred earlier while they were in the desert of Zin (v. 1); but it tells us why Moses did not enter the promise land of Canaan.

The congregation gathered against Moses and Aaron because there was no water for them. They asked, "Why have you brought up the congregation of the LORD into this wilderness, that we and our cattle should die?" (v. 4)

God instructed Moses, "Take the rod and gather the assembly together. Speak to the rock before their eyes; and it shall give forth its water." (vv. 7-8) "And Moses ... gathered the assembly together before the rock, and he said to them, 'Hear now, you rebels! Must we bring water for you out of this rock?' Then Moses lifted up his hand and struck the rock twice with his rod; and water came out abundantly." NKJV (Numbers 20:10-11)

However, God was not pleased with Moses, who had failed to obey God's instructions to "speak to the rock." Instead, he struck the rock as he had done earlier to get water. At that time God had instructed Moses to "strike the rock, and water will come out of it." (Exodus 17:1-7) But this time, God told Moses to "speak to the rock." Instead of obeying God, Moses spoke to the people and failed to give praise to God for the water. Because of his disobedience, God did not allow Moses to enter into the land of Canaan. (Numbers 20:12)

God had a reason for striking the rock only on the first occasion when they needed water. (Exodus 17:1-7) We read in the New Testament, "They drank of that spiritual Rock that followed them, and that Rock was Christ. ...

Now all these things happened to them for examples; and were written for our admonition." (1 Cor. 10:1-11) Water is a symbol for life. (John 4:10-14) Jesus Christ is our Rock who gives us life; and "Christ was offered once to bear the sins of many." (Hebrews 9:28; 10:9-10,14) Now, we are to speak to him. (John 16:24) Also, we are not under the old covenant of Moses; we are to obey the new covenant of Christ.

> **They did not destroy the nations,**
> **concerning whom the LORD commanded them;**
> **But were mingled among the heathen,**
> **and learned their works.**
> **And they served their idols,**
> **which were a snare to them.**
> **Yes, they sacrificed their sons and their daughters**
> **unto devils.**
> **And shed innocent blood,**
> **even the blood of their sons and daughters,**
> **whom they sacrificed to the idols of Canaan;**
> **And the land was polluted with blood.**
> **Thus, they were defiled with their own works,**
> **And went a-whoring with their own inventions.**
> **106:34-39**

God had commanded them with a promise: "I will deliver the inhabitants of the land into your hand; and you shall drive them out before you. You shall make no covenant with them, nor with their gods. They shall not dwell in your land, lest they make you sin against me; for if you serve their gods, it will surely be a snare to you." (Exodus 23:31-33) The tribe of Benjamin shared their land with the Jebusites (Judges 1:21). Canaanites lived with the tribes of Manasseh, Ephraim, Zebulun, Asher and Naphtali. (Judges 1:27-33) The Amorites lived in the land that belonged to the tribe of Dan (Judges 34-36). God said, "You have not obeyed my voice. Why have you done this?" (Judges 2:2) They had their own interests.

After the death of Joshua, the Israelites worshiped the gods of the peoples around them. They served Baal and the Ashtoreth. (Judges 2:8-13) Later, even Solomon also worshiped these gods, including Molech. (1 Kings 11:5-7) Ahaz, king of Judah, "burnt his children in the fire after the abominations of the heathen." (2 Chronicles 28:1-3) Ahaz's grandson, Manasseh, "seduced them (the Jews) to do evil more than the nations whom the LORD destroyed before the sons of Israel." NASB (2 Kings 21:9)

The LORD said that the city of Jerusalem had forsaken him by sacrificing to other gods and shedding "the blood of the innocents." He accused them of burning their sons with fire as burnt offerings to Baal. (Jer. 19:3-5) "The attractiveness of this worship (of Baal) to the Jews undoubtedly grew out of its licentious character." [4] The act of "shedding innocent blood" in abortion clinics is due to the sexual permissiveness in our culture. This sin was one of the reasons God allowed Jerusalem to be destroyed. (Jer. 19:6-15)

> **Therefore, the wrath of the LORD was kindled**
> **against his people,**
> **Insomuch that he abhorred his own inheritance.**
> **And he gave them into the hand of the heathen;**
> **And they that hated them ruled over them.**
> **Their enemies also oppressed them,**
> **And they were brought into subjection**
> **under their hand.**
> **Many times, he did deliver them;**
> **But they provoked him with their counsel,**
> **And were brought low for their iniquity. 106:40-43**

God punished his people for their sins with invading nations that oppressed them. They desired to worship the idols of the heathen; so, God let the heathen rule over them from time to time.

---

[4] F. N. Peloubet, *Peloubet's Bible Dictionary,* p. 64

Nevertheless, He regarded their affliction,
when he heard their cry;
And for their sake He remembered His covenant,
And relented according to the multitude
of His mercies,
He also made them to be pitied
by all those who carried them away captive. NKJV
106:44-46

God had promised the Israelites that if they would keep his commandments, he would give them blessings and peace. But if they disobeyed him, they would suffer natural calamities and they would be oppressed by enemies. God said, "I will bring the land into desolation. And I will scatter you among the heathen. Then the land shall enjoy her sabbaths. As long as it lies desolate it shall rest." If they would humble themselves and confess their iniquity, God promised to hear their cry and remember His covenant with their fathers, Abraham, Isaac and Jacob. (Lev. 26:1-46) God's people who had been taken captive by the Assyrians and Babylonians were pitied and allowed to return to Jerusalem to rebuild God's temple. (Ezra 1:1-3)

Save us, O LORD, our God,
And gather us from among the heathen,
To give thanks unto thy holy name,
And to triumph in thy praise. 106:47

This psalm began with praise to the LORD, who had shown mercy to His people. He had restored them to their homeland. (vv. 1-5) It closes with a prayer that God would continue to gather them from among the nations.

Psalms Book Four concludes with these words:
Blessed be the LORD God of Israel
from everlasting to everlasting;
And let all the people say, "Amen!"
Praise the LORD. 106:47

NOTES

PSALMS

Book Five

Ezra's Collection of Psalms

Psalms 107 – 150

Ezra the scribe made this collection of forty-four psalms after the return from exile. David wrote fifteen of these psalms: 108, 109, 110, 122, 124, 131, 133, 138, 139, 140, 141, 142, 143, 144 and 145. Solomon wrote Psalm 127. The writers of the other 28 psalms are not known. Psalm 119 is the longest psalm; it has 176 verses that emphasize the importance of the Holy Scriptures. Psalm 117 has only two verses, and it tells all nations to praise the LORD. Many instructional psalms are found in Book Five.

Psalm 107

Give Thanks for God's Providential Care

This psalm may have been written for the Feast of the Tabernacles after the Jews had returned to Jerusalem. God had gathered them out of foreign lands. (vv. 2-3,14) **"Oh, that men would give thanks to the LORD for His goodness, and for His wonderful works to the children of men!"** NKJV (verses 8, 16, 21 & 31)

> **Oh, give thanks unto the LORD, for He is good!**
> **For his mercy endures forever.**
> **Let the redeemed of the LORD say so,**
> **Whom he has redeemed from the hand of the enemy,**
> **And gathered them out of the lands,**
> **From the east and from the west,**
> **From the north and from the south. 107:1-3**

The LORD had redeemed his people who had been scattered by the nations. He now is redeeming his people, Christians, who have been in the bondage of Satan and sin; and he is gathering them from all over the earth. The redeemed are to give thanks to the LORD, their Redeemer.

> **They wandered in the wilderness in a solitary way;**
> **They found no city to dwell in.**
> **Hungry and thirsty,**
> **Their soul fainted in them.**
> **Then they cried unto the LORD in their trouble,**
> **And he delivered them out of their distresses.**
> **And he led them forth by the right way,**
> **That they might go to a city of habitation.**
> **Oh, that men would praise the LORD for his goodness,**
> **And for his wonderful works to the children of men!**
> **For he satisfies the longing soul,**
> **And fills the hungry soul with goodness. 107:4-9**

Their time in exile was like a people wandering in a desolate desert— hungry and thirsty. Their soul fainted as they looked for a place to live. They prayed to the LORD, and he brought them to the city of Jerusalem. He satisfied the longing of their soul.

The Christian's present life on earth is like God's people in their exile. If we seek the LORD, he will deliver us from our distresses and take us to our home in heaven.

> Those who sat in darkness
>   and in the shadow of death,
> Bound in affliction and irons—
> Because they rebelled against the words of God,
> And despised the counsel of the Most High.
> Therefore He brought down their heart with labor;
> They fell down, and there was none to help.
> Then they cried out to the LORD in their trouble,
> And He saved them out of their distresses.
> He brought them out of darkness and the shadow
>   of death,
> And broke their chains in pieces.
> Oh, that men would give thanks to the LORD
>   for His goodness,
> And for His wonderful works to the children of men!
> For He has broken the gates of bronze,
> And cut the bars of iron in two. 107:10-16 NKJV

The exile of God's people is described as a prisoner sitting in darkness awaiting death. They were suffering distresses because that had rebelled against God's words and despised his advice. Many people are suffering today for the same reason. God saved the Jews when they cried out to Him. God had promised over a hundred years earlier, "I will break in pieces the gates of bronze and cut the bars of iron" in order to restore his people to their homeland (Isaiah 45:2) and to rebuild Jerusalem and the temple. (Isaiah 44:28)

Fools, because of their transgression,
And because of their iniquities, were afflicted.
Their soul abhorred all manner of food,
And they drew near to the gates of death.
Then they cried out to the LORD in their trouble,
And He saved them out of their distresses.
He sent His word and healed them,
And delivered them from their destructions.
Oh, that men would give thanks to the LORD
   for His goodness,
And for His wonderful works to the children of men!
Let them sacrifice the sacrifices of thanksgiving,
And declare His works with rejoicing. 107:17-22 NKJV

The Feast of Tabernacles was the Jewish festival of thanksgiving. The Day of Atonement came five days before their thanksgiving. The people confessed their sins, and sacrifices were made for them. Before the Jews could return to their homeland, they had to confess their sins and seek the LORD. (Jeremiah 29:10-14) While they were in exile, it appeared that the nation of Israel would die and be no more. But God restored his nation.

Those who go down to the sea in ships,
Who do business on the great waters,
They see the works of the LORD,
And His wonders in the deep.
For He commands and raises the stormy wind,
Which lifts up the waves of the sea.
They mount up to the heavens,
They go down again to the depths;
The soul melts because of trouble.
They reel to and fro,
And stagger like a drunken man,
And are at their wits' end.
Then they cry out to the LORD in their trouble,
And He brings them out of their distresses.
He calms the storm
So that its waves are still.

Then they are glad because they are quiet;
So He guides them to their desired haven.
Oh, that men would give thanks to the LORD
    for His goodness,
And for His wonderful works to the children of men!
Let them exalt Him also in the assembly of the people,
And praise Him in the company of the elders. ^{NKJV}

107:23-32

God's people in exile are like those who go to sea in ships. God commands the storms that blow the waves that lift their boats high up and then low down; they are tossed about by the storm. When things seem hopeless, they cry out to God; and he calms the storm. This reminds us of when Jesus calmed the storm while in a boat on the Sea of Galilee. And his disciples said to each other: "What manner of man is this, that even the wind and the sea obey him?" (Mark 8:36-41) We should see God's providential care for us; and give thanks to Him.

He turned rivers into a desert,
    flowing springs into thirsty ground,
and fruitful land into a salty waste,
    because of the wickedness of those who lived there.
He turned the desert into pools of water
    and the parched ground into flowing springs;
there he brought the hungry to live,
    and they founded a city where they could settle.
They sowed fields and planted vineyards
    that yielded a fruitful harvest;
he blessed them, and their numbers greatly increased,
    and he did not let their herds diminish. ^{NIV}

107:33-38

God allowed the armies of Babylon to destroy the homeland of the Jews. A fruitful land became a salty waste land, because of the wickedness of the Jews. While in exile, the Jews repented and prayed to God; and the LORD turned that deserted and parched land into flowing springs of water. He brought his hungry people back to their homeland to live and rebuild the city of Jerusalem. Their fields and vineyards produced a fruitful harvest. Their people and cattle increased in numbers.

> **When they are diminished and brought low**
> **through oppression, affliction and sorrow,**
> **He pours contempt on princes,**
> **and causes them to wander in the wilderness**
> **where there is no way;**
> **Yet He sets the poor on high, far from affliction,**
> **and makes their families like a flock.**
> **The righteous see it and rejoice,**
> **And all iniquity stops its mouth. 107:39-42** NKJV

God's people forsook him and worshiped idols. The Assyrians and Babylonians destroyed their cities, towns and farms; and many of them died. God poured contempt upon the rulers of Israel who had forsaken him; and they spent many years of oppression, calamity and sorrow while in exile. When the LORD restored his faithful people to Jerusalem, they saw his blessings and rejoiced. The wicked saw God's power, and they were speechless.

> **Whoever is wise, let him heed these things**
> **and consider the great love of the LORD.** NIV
> **107:43**

Are we listening? God is working providentially either to discipline us or to bless us. He is in control of nature. He sent a great flood in the days of Noah that covered the earth, because of man's wickedness. He has sent famine and pestilence. (Jeremiah 21:9) He is in control of the rise and fall of nations. Are we considering the LORD's great power and love? Are we being faithful to him? The wise will hear and obey the words of God. They will not rebel against the LORD. They will not despise his counsel.

Psalm 108

God's Help over Enemies

A Song, A Psalm of David

Two years after the Jews had returned to Jerusalem, they laid the foundation for the new temple in 534 BC. But work on the temple ceased due to the Samaritans. Fourteen years later, God sent Haggai and Zechariah to encourage the Jews to finish building his new temple. (Ezra 3-5) Psalm 108 may have been written at this time. It ends with a prayer: "Give us help from trouble." ^{NKJV} The first five verses are from David's Psalm 57:7-11, and verses 6-13 are from his Psalm 60:5-12.

> **O God, my heart is fixed;**
> **I will sing and give praise, even with my glory.**
> **Awake, psaltery and harp!**
> **I will awake early.**
> **I will praise thee, O LORD, among the people,**
> **And I will sing praises to you among the nations.**
> **For thy mercy is great above the heavens,**
> **And thy glory above all the earth.**
> **Be thou exalted, O God, above the heavens,**
> **And thy glory above all the earth. 108:1-5**

> **That thy beloved may be delivered,**
> **Save with thy right hand, and answer me.**
> **God has spoken in his holiness:**
> **"I will rejoice.**
> **I will divide Shechem**
> **And measure out the valley of Succoth.**
> **Gilead is mine; Manasseh is mine;**
> **Ephraim also is the strength of my head;**
> **Judah is my lawgiver;**
> **Moab is my wash pot;**
> **Over Edom I will cast out my shoe;**
> **Over Philistia I will triumph."**

Who will bring me into the strong city?
Who will lead me into Edom?
Will not thou, O God,
   who has cast us off?
And will not thou, O God,
   go forth with our hosts?
Give us help from trouble,
For vain is the help of man.
Through God we shall do valiantly,
For He it is that shall tread down our enemies.
                     108:6-13

These psalms of David may have encouraged the Jews to build God's temple. May we apply the psalms to our current needs and conditions as we serve the LORD.

Psalm 109

A Plea for God to Take Vengeance

A Psalm of David

In this psalm, David says, "I am poor and needy, and my heart is wounded within me. I am gone like the shadow." (vv. 22-23) Read Psalm 41, which describes David's enemies speaking lies of hate against him and rejoicing over his being sick and near death. David, being a prophet, wanted to hear from God (Acts 2:29-30), but the LORD had revealed nothing to him during this time.

Do not be silent, O God of my praise!
For the mouth of the wicked and the mouth of
   the deceitful have opened against me;
They have spoken against me with a lying tongue.
They have also surrounded me with words of hatred,
And fought against me without cause.
In return for my love they are my accusers,
But I give myself to prayer.
Thus, they have rewarded me evil for good.
And hatred for my love. **109:1-5** NKJV

David is describing the conditions when Absalom's rebellion was forming. Many of David's close associates did not remain loyal to him. They spoke deceitful and hateful words against him. David's close counselor and friend was Ahithophel, but he joined the rebellion against David. He repaid David "evil for good" and "hatred for love." An imprecatory psalm is in verses 6-20, and for the most part it is against Ahithophel.

> **Appoint a wicked man over him;**
> **And let an accuser stand at his right hand.**
> **When he is judged, let him come forth guilty;**
> **And let his prayer become sin.**
> **Let his days be few;**
> **Let another take his office.**
> **Let his children be fatherless, and his wife a widow.**
> **Let his children wander about and beg;**
> **And let them seek *sustenance* far from**
> **their ruined homes.**
> **Let the creditors seize all that he has;**
> **And let his posterity be cut off;**
> **In a following generation let their name be**
> **blotted out. 109:6-13** NASB

David's prayer was answered. Hushai was appointed Absalom's counselor instead of Ahithophel. (2 Samuel 17:14) David's request for another to "take his office" (v.8) was fulfilled. Because Absalom had rejected him, Ahithophel hanged himself. (2 Samuel 17:23)

This psalm is typically prophetic of the punishment of those who would reject Christ. In Acts 1:20, Peter quoted this psalm in verse 8, "Let another take his office." Another man had to be appointed an apostle in the place of Judas, who had betrayed Jesus, and then he hanged himself. Judas was like Ahithophel. This imprecatory psalm declares the punishment of those who reject the Christ, as we will see in Psalm 110.

Let the iniquity of his fathers
     be remembered with the LORD;
And let not the sin of his mother
     be blotted out.
Let them be before the LORD continually,
That he may cut off the memory of them
     from the earth.
Because he remembered not to show mercy,
But persecuted the poor and needy man,
That he might slay the broken in heart.
As he loved cursing, so let it come unto him;
As he delighted not in blessing,
     so let it be far from him.
As he clothed himself with cursing as with his garment,
So let it come into his bowels like water,
     and like oil into his bones.
Let it be unto him as the garment which covers him,
And for a girdle wherewith he is girded continually.
Let this be the reward of my adversaries
     from the LORD,
And of them that speak evil against my soul. **109:14-20**

Christians are instructed in Romans 12:19 not to avenge themselves, because vengeance belongs to the LORD; he will repay wrongdoers. David is calling upon God to take vengeance as he has promised.

But you, O GOD, my Lord,
     deal on my behalf for your name's sake;
     because your steadfast love is good, deliver me!
For I am poor and needy,
     and my heart is stricken within me.
I am gone like a shadow at evening;
     I am shaken off like a locust.
My knees are weak through fasting;
     my body has become gaunt, with no fat.
I am an object of scorn to my accusers;
     when they see me, they wag their heads.

Help me, O LORD, my God!
Save me according to your steadfast love!
Let them know that this is your hand;
    you, O LORD, have done it!
Let them curse, but you will bless!
They arise and put to shame,
    but your servant will be glad!
May my accusers be clothed with dishonor;
May they be wrapped in their own shame
    as in a cloak! 109:26-29 ESV

When David was restored to his throne in Jerusalem, everyone knew that the hand of the LORD had done it. When Jesus was raised from the dead to sit on his throne, thousands knew it was by God's power. (Acts 2;22-41)

I will greatly praise the LORD with my mouth;
Yes, I will praise him among the multitude.
For he shall stand at the right hand of the poor,
To save him from those that condemn his soul.
                        109:30-31

Psalm 110

The Reign of The Messiah

A Psalm of David

This prophetic psalm predicts the reign of the Messiah. David wrote about God's victories over our adversaries in Psalms 108, 109 and 110. In the New Testament, Psalm 110 is quoted more often than any other psalm.

The LORD said to my Lord,
"Sit at my right hand,
    until I make your enemies your footstool."
The LORD shall send the rod of thy strength
    out of Zion;
Rule in the midst of your enemies." 110:1-2

This psalm is an oracle of God. The LORD (*Yahweh*) is speaking to David's Lord (*Adoni*), the supreme ruler—the Messiah. In Matthew 22:41-46, Jesus quoted from this psalm to prove that the Messiah would be more than the son of David; he would be David's Lord.

"The rod" (scepter) of Christ's power that went out of Zion in Jerusalem was the gospel of Christ. It was revealed and confirmed by the Holy Spirit. (John 14:26, John 16:12-14, Acts 1:8 and Acts 2:1-4) This gospel is the power of God to save us. (Romans 1:16) The last enemy that he will destroy is death. (1 Cor. 15:25-26)

On Pentecost, Peter quoted Psalm 110:1 and said, "Therefore, let all the house of Israel know assuredly that God has made that same Jesus, whom you have crucified, both Lord and Christ." (Acts 2:34-36).

> **Thy people shall be willing in the day of your power;**
> **In the beauties of holiness**
> > **from the womb of the morning,**
> **You have the dew of thy youth. 110:3**

The people in Christ's kingdom would willingly serve him. When the gospel was preached for the first time, three-thousand souls "gladly received" it. (Acts 2:37-41) The followers of Christ were like the refreshing dew.

> **The LORD has sworn**
> > **and will not change his mind:**
> **"You are a priest forever**
> > **in the order of Melchizedek." 110:4** NIV

God would keep his promise that the Messiah would be like Melchizedek, who was both a king and the priest of God (Genesis 14:18-20). Christ is both our king and our high priest. (Hebrews 6:19-20; 7:1-28) Melchizedek means "king of righteousness." And he was also the king of Salem, meaning "king of peace." (Hebrews 7:1-2)

> **The Lord is at Your right hand**
> **He will shatter kings in the day of His wrath.**
> **He will judge among the nations,**
> **He will fill *them* with corpses,**
> **He will shatter the chief men over a broad country.**
> **He will drink from the brook by the wayside;**
> **Therefore He will lift up *His* head. 110:5-7** ^{NASB}

Christ is at God's right hand to carry out the heavenly Father's will. Jesus said, "He who sent me is with me; the Father has not left me alone; for I always do those things that please him." (John 8:29) On Judgment Day, Christ will destroy the kings and judge the nations. (Matthew 25:31-46) He will "judge the living and the dead." (2 Tim. 4:1) "For we must all appear before the judgment seat of Christ." (2 Cor. 5:10) The **corpses** represent those who are slain by the spiritual sword that proceeds out of the mouth of Christ. (Rev. 19:15-18) "For the word of God is living and powerful, and sharper than any two-edged sword." ^{NKJV} (Heb. 4:12) The Messiah will refresh himself, and he will lift up his head in victory!

Psalm 111

Praise the LORD for His Wonderful Works

Praise the LORD!

> **I will praise the LORD with my whole heart,**
> **In the assembly of the upright**
> **and in the congregation. 111:1**

When we come together to worship God, each one of us should praise the LORD with our whole heart. Our thoughts, feelings and emotions must be centered on God and his wonderful works.

> **The works of the LORD are great,**
> **Studied by all who have pleasure in them.**

His work is honorable and glorious,
And His righteousness endures forever.
He has made His wonderful works
    to be remembered;
The LORD is gracious and full of compassion.
He has given food to those who fear Him.
He will ever be mindful of His covenant.
He has declared to His people
    the power of His works,
In giving them the heritage of the nations. NKJV

111:2-6

The wonderful works of the LORD are recorded in the Holy Scriptures. Those who want to know the LORD will study the Bible. We are to remember God's works, which reveal his righteousness, grace and compassion. He fed Israel with manna from heaven when they were in the wilderness. When Samaria was besieged by the Syrians, the people were starving to death, but God provided food for them. (2 Kings 6:24 – 7:16) God in his providence still provides for our physical and spiritual needs. God kept his covenant with Abraham, Isaac and Jacob by giving the land of Canaan to the Israelites.

The works of his hands are truth and justice;
All his commandments are sure.
They stand fast forever and ever,
And are done in truth and uprightness.
He sent redemption to his people;
He has commanded his covenant forever:
Holy and reverend is his name. 111:7-9

All that God does is right. God's moral law stands the test of time. It is wrong to murder another human being. It is wrong to steal and to bear false witness. We are to honor our father and mother. God is able to redeem his people. Both "sanctified" and "holy" mean "set apart." God's name is to be "set apart" from all others. Only the LORD is to be called "Reverend." The root meaning of the word "reverend" means "to fear."

The fear of the LORD is the beginning of wisdom;
A good understanding
     have all those who do his commandments.
His praise endures forever. 111:10

"The fear of the LORD is the beginning of wisdom" is a well-known proverb. (Job 28:28; Proverbs 1:7 and 9:10) Solomon said, "Let us hear the conclusion of the whole matter: Fear God and keep his commandments." (Ecclesiastes 12:13) God's praise will not end.

Psalm 112

The LORD Blesses the Godly Man

Praise ye the LORD!

Blessed is the man who fears the LORD,
Who delights greatly in his commandments. 112:1

Psalms 111 and 112 go together; they are similar in form. Each psalm begins with "Praise ye the LORD" and has twenty-two lines divided into ten verses. "Each line begins with a successive letter of the Hebrew alphabet, from *alef* to *tau*, that is, from a to z." [5] Psalm 111 praises God for his works. Psalm 112 praises God for blessing the godly man. Compare Psalm 112 with Psalm 1.

His descendants will be mighty on earth;
The generation of the upright will be blessed.
Wealth and riches will be in his house,
And his righteousness endures forever.
Unto the upright there arises light in the darkness;
He is gracious, and full of compassion, and righteous.
A good man deals graciously and lends;
He will guide his affairs with discretion. 112:2-5 NKJV

---

[5] James Limburg, *Psalms,* p. 382

The children of a godly man will prosper. Following his example, they will be known for their virtue, success and influence for good. (This is a general rule; there will be some exceptions, according to Ezekiel 18:5-13.) In the house of the upright are "true riches." (1 Tim. 6:6,18)

The influence of a godly life continues long after death; for **his righteousness endures forever.** Think of godly men and women you have known who are now dead; but they are still serving as good examples for you to follow. From generation to generation, their righteous influence lives on. (Hebrews 11:4-16)

The godly have times of **darkness**—days of hardships. Jesus said, "In the world you will have tribulation; but be of good cheer. I have overcome the world." (John 16:33) God's word is "a light" for us. (Psalm 119:105) "For God … has shined in our hearts to give the light of the glory of God in the face of Jesus Christ." (2 Cor. 4:6) "Endure hardship as discipline; God is treating you as sons." NIV (Heb. 12:7-11) Discipline is for our good. (James 1:2-5)

The upright person is described as being "gracious and full of compassion" in verse 4. The same words are used to describe the LORD in 111:4. As God's children, we are to be like our Father. "We all … beholding as in a mirror the glory of the Lord, are being transformed into the same image from glory to glory." NKJV (2 Cor. 3:18) The godly have compassion for the poor and lend to those in need with good judgment.

> **Surely he will never be shaken;**
> **The righteous will be in everlasting remembrance.**
> **He will not be afraid of evil tidings;**
> **His heart is steadfast, trusting in the LORD.**
> **His heart is established;**
> **He will not be afraid,**
> **Until he sees his desire upon his enemies. 112:6-8** NKJV

The godly person is not shaken in his faith regardless of the circumstances, because he knows the Lord has promised, "I will never leave you, nor forsake you." So, the godly may boldly say, "The Lord is my helper, and I will not fear what man will do." (Heb. 13:5-6) His trust in the Lord secures his heart. His eyes are fixed "on Jesus, the author and perfector of our faith." NIV (Heb. 12:2-3)

> **He has dispersed abroad,**
> **He has given to the poor;**
> **His righteousness endures forever;**
> **His horn will be exalted with honor.**
> **The wicked will see it and be grieved;**
> **He will gnash his teeth and melt away.**
> **The desire of the wicked shall perish. 112:9-10** NKJV

The wicked will come to grief and destruction when they see the honor and strength of the upright. "For the LORD knows the way of the righteous; but the way of the ungodly shall perish." (Psalm 1:6)

Psalm 113

The Almighty is Mindful of the Lowly

Psalms 113-118 were sung together as a grand hymn of praise at the three great feast days and on other special days. During the Passover supper in the Jewish homes, these psalms were sung. Psalm 113 reminds us that the LORD cares for the needy and the lowly.

> **Praise ye the LORD!**
> **Praise, O ye servants of the LORD,**
> **Praise the name of the LORD.**
> **Blessed be the name of the LORD,**
> **From this time forth and forevermore!**
> **From the rising of the sun**
> **to the going down of the same,**
> **The LORD's name is to be praised. 113:1-3**

The LORD's servants are to praise him. Those who had been scattered by the Assyrians and Babylonians were to return to the restored temple in Jerusalem for the great feast days. (Acts 2:1,5) The **name** of the LORD is to be praised. His name refers to his almighty power, his wisdom, his truth, his justice, his loving kindness and mercy. **Blessed be the name of the LORD.** These words inspired W. H. Clark to write the following words in a hymn for us to sing today:

> All praise to Him who reigns above,
> In majesty supreme;
> Who gave His Son for man to die,
> That He might man redeem.
> Blessed be the name, blessed be the name,
> Blessed be the name of the Lord.

The LORD's name is to be praised throughout the entire earth and in heaven forevermore. Malachi 1:11 refers to Psalm 113:3, saying, "From the rising of the sun even to the going down of the same, my name shall be great among the Gentiles."

> **The LORD is high above all nations,**
> **And his glory above the heavens.**
> **Who is like the LORD our God,**
> **Who dwells on high,**
> **Who humbles himself**
> > **to behold the things that are in heaven**
> > **and in the earth? 113:5-6**

The LORD's power is supreme. He rules over all the nations on earth and governs the universe. No being is like the LORD our God. He dwells on high! The LORD says, "Heaven is my throne, and the earth is my footstool." (Isaiah 66:1) Yet, the LORD humbles himself and looks down to the earth in order to help those who are in need. This humility is seen in Jesus. (Phil. 2:5-11)

> He raises up the poor out of the dust,
> And lifts the needy out of the dunghill;
> That he may set him with princes,
> Even with the princes of his people.
> He makes the barren woman to keep house,
> And to be a joyful mother of children.

Praise the LORD! 113:7-9

The LORD lifted Joseph out of slavery and prison and made him a ruler in Egypt. He took the baby, Moses, from the Nile River and eventually made him the one who would deliver his people from their slavery in Egypt. He took a shepherd, David, and made him king of Israel. He took a captive, Daniel, and made him an advisor to kings of two different kingdoms. Even in our own time, we know of great men whom God has lifted up from humble beginnings to high places of responsibility.

The LORD has also made "joyful" mothers. Children were born to several barren women—Sarah, Rebekah, Rachel, Hannah and Elisabeth. Hannah was the mother of the great prophet Samuel. John the Baptist was the son of Elisabeth, and Jesus Christ is a descendant of Sarah. The world has been blessed, because God answered the prayers of these women.

We should praise the LORD!

Psalm 114

The Deliverance of Israel

God's deliverance of the nation of Israel from Egypt was celebrated during the feast of Passover.

> When Israel went out of Egypt,
> The house of Jacob from a people of strange language,
> Judah became His sanctuary,
> And Israel his dominion. **114:1-2**

This psalm was written to encourage the Jews as they returned to Jerusalem to restore God's kingdom. While in exile, they heard a foreign language that reminded them that their fathers also had heard a strange language in Egypt. Judah became the **sanctuary** of God, when the temple was built. Israel became the **dominion** of God. A sea, a river, mountains and hills are poetically personified in this psalm to describe how Israel became the kingdom of the LORD.

> **The sea saw it and fled; Jordan was driven back.**
> **The mountains skipped like rams,**
> **And the little hills like lambs.**
> **What ailed thee, O thou sea, that you fled?**
> **Thou Jordan, that you were driven back?**
> **Ye mountains, that ye skipped like rams?**
> **And ye little hills, like lambs? 114:3-6**

The Red Sea parted allowing the people of Israel to be saved from the Egyptian army. (Exodus 14:15-30) The Israelites crossed the flooded Jordan River on dry ground into Canaan because the river was driven back. (Joshua 3:14-17) When the Law was given to Israel on Mount Sinai, the mountain and its hills trembled with an earthquake. (Exodus 19:18-20:18) What caused all of these things? The power of the LORD is the answer.

> **Tremble, O earth, at the presence of the LORD,**
> **At the presence of the God of Jacob,**
> **Who turned the rock into a pool of water,**
> **The flint into a fountain of waters. 114:7-8** NKJV

The LORD gave Jacob the name **Israel**, which means **power with God**. As Jacob's descendants, the Israelites had God's power with them. When they got thirsty in the wilderness, the LORD gave them water from a rock on two occasions. We all should tremble with reverence because we are in the presence of the LORD.

Psalm 115

Trust in the LORD

Those who have power with God are the true Israel. Glory belongs to our God for all of his divine attributes. The people of Israel are instructed three times in this psalm to "trust in the LORD." (vv. 9-11)

> **Not unto us, O LORD, not unto us,**
> **But unto thy name give glory,**
> **For thy mercy,**
> **And for thy truth's sake. 115:1**

When we accomplish great things and do good deeds, we may forget that God is the one who gave us the power and the abilities to do these things. Paul asked Christians, "What do you have that you did not receive? Now if you did receive it, why do you boast as if you had not received it?" NKJV (1 Cor. 4:7) "He who glories, let him glory in the LORD." NKJV (1 Cor. 1:31) We depend upon the LORD for our power and wisdom and for his blessings. All the glory belongs to him. "Our sufficiency is from God." NKJV (2 Corinthians 3:5)

> **Why should the nations say,**
> **"Where, now, is their God?"**
> **But our God is in the heavens;**
> **He does whatever He pleases. 115:2-3** NASB

When the temple of the LORD and the city of Jerusalem lay in ruins for many years, the other nations were saying, "Where, now, is their God?" It appeared that God was powerless to save his people and his lands. But the Jews would answer, "Our God is in the heavens, and he carries out his purposes." The LORD called for the destruction of Jerusalem because of its sins; and he appointed Cyrus to call for the rebuilding of Jerusalem and the temple. (Read Isaiah 2:17 – 3:26 and 44:28 – 45:6.)

> Their idols are silver and gold,
>   the work of men's hands.
> They have mouths, but they speak not;
>   eyes, but they see not;
> They have ears, but they hear not;
>   noses, but they smell not;
> They have hands, but they handle not;
>   feet, but they walk not;
> Neither speak they through their throat.
> They who make them are like them;
> So is everyone who trusts in them. 115:4-8

The pagan idols may be seen, but they are useless. The makers of images and their worshipers are not blessed.

> O Israel, trust in the LORD;
> He is their help and their shield.
> O house of Aaron, trust in the LORD;
> He is their help and their shield.
> You who fear the LORD, trust in the LORD;
> He is their help and their shield. 115:9-11

The LORD has the power to provide and to protect. Those who are called to **trust in the LORD** are: (1) the nation of Israel, (2) the priests of Aaron's family, and (3) God-fearing Gentiles who worshiped the LORD in the synagogues of the Jews. (Acts 13:14-16,26,42)

In the new covenant of Christ, Christians are God's "holy nation," his "royal priesthood" and "his own special people." We are to "proclaim the praises of Him who called (us) out of darkness into His marvelous light: who once were not a people but are now the people of God." NKJV (1 Peter 2:9-10) We are to **trust in the LORD**.

> The LORD has been mindful of us;
> He will bless us;
> He will bless the house of Israel;
> He will bless the house of Aaron.
> He will bless those who fear the LORD,
> Both small and great. 115:12-13

L. O. Sanderson wrote the hymn, "The Lord Has Been Mindful of Me." It was likely inspired by verse 12 of this psalm. The words of the chorus are:

> "The Lord has been mindful of me!
> He blesses and blesses again!
> My God is the God of the living!
> How excellent is His name!"

Psalm 8:4 asks the LORD, "What is man, that thou art mindful of him?" He knows our physical and spiritual needs, and he gives us all those things that we need. (Matthew 6:31-33; 1 Cor. 12:7-9) We are truly blessed!

> **The LORD shall increase you more and more,**
> **you and your children.**
> **You are blessed of the LORD,**
> **who made heaven and earth.**
> **The heaven, even the heavens, are the LORD's;**
> **But the earth he has given to the children of men.**
> **115:14-16**

True Israel consists of those who worship the LORD, who is the creator of the heavens. He has richly provided a dwelling-place for mankind—the earth! "He gave us rain from heaven and fruitful seasons, filling our hearts with food and gladness." (Acts 14:17) But many have "worshiped and served created things rather than the Creator." ᴺᴵⱽ (Romans 1:25)

> **The dead praise not the LORD,**
> **Neither any that go down into silence.**
> **But we will bless the LORD**
> **From this time forth and forevermore.**
> **Praise the LORD. 115:17-18**

The worldly-minded are spiritually dead. (1 Tim. 5:6) If we do not praise the LORD during our life on earth, it will be too late to praise him after we die. (Hebrews 9:27) So, praise the LORD now and forever!

Psalm 116

Thanksgiving for Deliverance

According to an old Hebrew tradition, this psalm was written by king Hezekiah when the LORD delivered him from death as described in Isaiah 38. [6] The Assyrian army had conquered the northern kingdom of Israel and was then threatening the city of Jerusalem. The prophet Isaiah came to Hezekiah and said, **"Thus says the LORD, 'Set your house in order; for you shall die and not live.'"** Hezekiah prayed to the LORD and wept bitterly. This king had restored the worship of the LORD in the temple after destroying idolatry. Hezekiah was concerned about his nation. Would Jerusalem and God's people be destroyed? God heard his prayers, and he said to him, *"I will add to your days fifteen years. And I will deliver you and this city out of the hand of the king of Assyria, and I will defend this city."* (Isaiah 38:1-6) God kept this promise. (Isaiah 37:33-37)

> **I love the LORD, because he has heard**
> **My voice and my supplications.**
> **Because he has inclined his ear to me,**
> **Therefore, I will call upon him as long as I live.**
> **116:1-2**

The fact that God hears and answers prayers is one of the many reasons why we should love the LORD.

> **The cords of death entangled me,**
> **the anguish of the grave came upon me;**
> **I was overcome by trouble and sorrow.**
> **Then I called on the name of the LORD:**
> **"O LORD, save me!" 116:3-4** [NIV]

In his helplessness and tears, Hezekiah prayed to God for himself and for his nation.

---

[6] G. Rawlinson, *The Pulpit Commentary,* Vol. 8, *The Psalms,* p. 70

> The LORD is gracious and righteous;
>   our God is full of compassion.
> The LORD protects the simplehearted;
>   when I was in need, he saved me.
> Be at rest once more, O my soul,
>   for the LORD has been good to you. 116:5-7 NIV

Our God does that which is right, and he shows grace and mercy to us. He protects those who look to him with a childlike faith believing "the testimony of the LORD is sure." (Psalm 19:7) The simplehearted know that they need God. Knowing that God had saved him from death caused Hezekiah to believe that the LORD would save Jerusalem when it was besieged by 185,000 Assyrian soldiers. (Isaiah 37)

> For thou hast delivered my soul from death,
> My eyes from tears, and my feet from falling.
> I will walk before the LORD in the land of the living.
> I believed; therefore, I have spoken.
> I was greatly afflicted.
> I said in my haste, "All men are liars." 116:8-11

Because of his faith in God, Hezekiah prayed when he was afflicted with a deathly sickness and again when the Assyrians besieged Jerusalem. (2 Kings19:14-19) When the Assyrians took all the fortified cities of Judah, Hezekiah paid 300 talents of silver and 30 talents of gold to the king of Assyria in order to have peace. But, Sennacherib king of Assyria sent his army to besiege Jerusalem. (2 Kings 18:13-17) At that time, Hezekiah could have said, "All men are liars." Lying men are in contrast with the truthful Eternal One! When God healed Hezekiah of his deadly sickness, he also promised to deliver the city of Jerusalem out of the hand of the king of Assyria, and he did it. (Read 2 Kings 19:32 – 20:1)

> **What shall I render to the LORD**
> **for all his benefits toward me?**
> **I will take the cup of salvation,**
> **and call upon the name of the LORD.**
> **I will pay my vows to the LORD**
> **now in the presence of all his people. 116:12-14**

God's **benefits** included giving Hezekiah fifteen more years and sparing Jerusalem and Judah from destruction. Hezekiah gratefully received the blessing of salvation by praising God and by keeping his promises to him. Hezekiah was known as one who "trusted in the LORD God of Israel" and "held fast to the LORD." (2 Kings 18:5)

> **Precious in the sight of the LORD**
> *Is* **the death of his saints. 116:15**

A saint is one who is sanctified, dedicated to God. Paul asked Christians, "Do you not know that the unrighteous will not inherit the kingdom of God? … And such were some of you. But you were washed, but you were **sanctified**." NKJV (1 Cor. 9-11) All true followers of the LORD are his saints. The death of a Christian is precious to God. His saints will inherit the kingdom of heaven, and they will be with Him forever. "Blessed are the dead who die in the Lord … that they may rest from their labors and their works follow them." NKJV (Rev. 14:13)

> **O LORD, truly I am thy servant;**
> **I am thy servant, the son of your handmaid;**
> **Thou hast loosed my bonds.**
> **I will offer to you the sacrifice of thanksgiving,**
> **And I will call upon the name of the LORD.**
> **I will pay my vows to the LORD**
> **Now in the presence of all his people.**
> **In the courts of the LORD's house,**
> **In the midst of you, O Jerusalem.**
> **Praise ye the LORD. 116:16-19**

The closing words of Psalm 116 describe the thoughts of a dedicated servant of the LORD. Hezekiah is a good example for us to follow. Peter, Paul, James and Jude were the servants of Christ. (2 Peter 1:1; Romans 1:1; James 1:1 and Jude 1:1) As Christians, we should think of ourselves as the servants of God, because he has loosed us from the bondage of sin and death. (Romans 6:22-23) We are to offer praises of thanksgiving in the congregation of God's people "in the house of God, which is the church of the living God." (1 Timothy 3:15) We will praise God forever in the New Jerusalem in heaven. (Revelation 21)

When the nation of Israel was restored after being taken away by the Assyrians and Babylonians, the Jews included this psalm by Hezekiah in the collection that was used to celebrate the Passover—Psalms 113-118.[7] God had not only delivered his people from their bondage in Egypt but he also had delivered them from their apparent end as a nation. "The LORD stirred up the spirit of Cyrus king of Persia so that he made a proclamation throughout his kingdom: ... 'Who is among you of all His people? ... Let him go up to Jerusalem ... and build the house of the LORD God of Israel.'" (Ezra 1:1-3) NKJB

Psalm 117

O praise the LORD, all ye nations!
Praise him, all ye people!
For his merciful kindness is great toward us,
And the truth of the LORD endures forever.
Praise ye the LORD! 117:1-2

God's providential protection of the nation of Israel should cause all nations to proclaim the LORD's power and sovereignty. Will Hill wrote a hymn for Psalm 117.

---

[7] James Limburg, *Psalms,* p. 397

Psalm 118

The LORD's Mercy Endures Forever

This psalm was likely written for the dedication of the new temple in Jerusalem after the captivity. [8] It begins and ends with these words:

> **O give thanks unto the LORD, for he is good;**
> **Because his mercy endures forever. 118:1, 29**

We need "**the truth** of the LORD." (117:2) And we also need "**his mercy.**" God's truth and mercy are everlasting.

> **Let Israel now say,**
> **"His mercy endures forever."**
> **Let the house of Aaron now say,**
> **"His mercy endures forever."**
> **Let those who fear the LORD now say,**
> **"His mercy endures forever." 118:2-4** NKJV

Those going to the temple to worship the LORD needed to be aware of their need for his mercy and his love. The worshipers were the assembly of Israel, the priests of the family of Aaron and the God-fearers of other nations. Those of all nations were permitted to worship the LORD in the outer court of the temple. Compare these verses with Psalm 115:9-13. The LORD had said in Isaiah 56:7, *"My house shall be called a house of prayer for all nations."* Jesus quoted this verse in Mark 11:17.

> **I called upon the LORD in distress;**
> **The LORD answered me *and set me* in a large place.**
> **The LORD is on my side;**
> **I will not fear.**
> **What can man do to me? 118:5-6**

The words in verse six are used in Hebrews 13:6 to encourage Christians. God can set us free from distress.

---

[8] Keil and Delitzsch, *Commentary on the Old Testament.* Biblesoft

The LORD is on my side as my helper;
I shall look in triumph on those who hate me. 118:7 ESV

The apostle Paul asks, "If God is for us, who can be against us?" (Romans 8:31) He then asks rhetorically, "Who shall separate us from the love of Christ?" (8:35) And he concludes, "We are more than conquerors through him who loved us." (8:37)

It is better to trust in the LORD
   than to put confidence in man.
It is better to trust in the LORD
   than to put confidence in princes. 118:8-9

Human leaders will disappoint us; but we can always trust in the LORD. The LORD had stirred the spirit of Cyrus king of Persia to make the decree for rebuilding the temple of the LORD in the city of Jerusalem (Ezra 1:1-4), but some of the Persian rulers who followed him were influenced by the Samaritans to stop the construction of the temple. (Ezra 4-6) God sent his prophets Haggai and Zechariah to encourage his people to finish building the temple. The LORD said, "Not by might, nor by power, but by my Spirit." "The hands of Zerubbabel have laid the foundation of this house; his hands shall also finish it." (Zechariah 4:6,9)

All nations surrounded me,
But in the name of the LORD, I will destroy them.
They surrounded me,
Yes, they surrounded me;
But in the name of the LORD, I will destroy them.
They surrounded me like bees;
They were quenched like a fire of thorns;
For in the name of the LORD, I will destroy them.
You pushed me violently, that I might fall,
But the LORD helped me.
The LORD is my strength and song,
And He has become my salvation. 118:10-14 NKJV

These words are personifying the entire nation of Israel as an individual person. Hostile nations had surrounded Israel from its beginning as a nation in Canaan to the destruction of Jerusalem. Babylon was the last kingdom destroyed by the LORD, who "rules in the kingdom of men." (Daniel 4:17) Now that the nation of Israel had been restored and the LORD's temple rebuilt, worshipers would praise the LORD as their helper, strength and salvation! Christians are now called God's "holy nation" (1 Peter 2:9); and the church has been surrounded by opposition from its beginning. We are to praise the LORD for being our helper, strength and salvation!

> **The voice of rejoicing and salvation**
> **is in the tent of the righteous:**
> **The right hand of the LORD does valiantly.**
> **The right hand of the LORD is exalted;**
> **The right hand of the LORD does valiantly.**
> **I shall not die, but live,**
> **And declare the works of the LORD.**
> **The LORD has chastened me severely,**
> **But he has not given me over unto death. 118:15-18**

The Assyrians had destroyed the kingdom of Israel and the Babylonians had destroyed the kingdom of Judah. But God gave them a spiritual resurrection from the dead. (Ezekiel 37:1-14) He caused Cyrus king of Persia to make a decree, saying, "Who is there among you **of all his people**? Let him go up to Jerusalem, and build the house of the LORD God of Israel." (Ezra 1:1-3)

> **Open to me the gates of righteousness;**
> **I will go through them, and I will praise the LORD.**
> **This is the gate of the LORD,**
> **Through which the righteous shall enter.**
> **I will praise You,**
> **For You have answered me,**
> **And have become my salvation. 118:19-21** NKJV

The gates of righteousness are the gates of the temple, "through which access is gained to the sanctuary of him (the LORD) who alone is truly righteous and the source of all righteousness in others." [9] One enters the gates to praise the LORD, our Savior.

> **The stone which the builders refused**
> > **has become the head stone of the corner.**
> **This is the LORD's doing;**
> > **it is marvelous in our eyes.**
> **This is the day which the LORD has made;**
> > **we will rejoice and be glad in it. 118:22-24**

Zerubbabel laid the foundation for the new temple in 534 BC. (Ezra 3:8-13) This foundation included the head cornerstone. But the builders refused to continue their work in building the temple for fifteen years because of opposition. (Ezra 4) It looked like the new temple would never be built. However, God's prophets Haggai and Zechariah encouraged the builders to resume their work in 520 BC, and the temple was completed four years later. The LORD had made possible this day of rejoicing! (Ezra 6:14-16) These events served as a metaphor of Israel, which was rejected and dead by men, but became the cornerstone to rebuild God's nation and complete his plan to bring the Messiah into the world. The Christ also would be rejected by men, but he would become the chief cornerstone of the LORD's spiritual temple, the church. (1 Peter 2:4-7)

> **Save now, I beseech thee, O LORD;**
> **I beseech thee, send now prosperity.**
> **Blessed is he who comes in the name of the LORD;**
> **We have blessed you from the house of the LORD.**
> **God is the LORD, who has shown us light;**
> **Bind the sacrifice with cords even to**
> > **the horns of the altar.**

---

[9] G. Rawlinson, *The Pulpit Commentary,* Vol. 8, *The Psalms,* p. 89

Thou art my God, and I will praise thee;
Thou art my God. I will exalt thee. 118:25-28

The benediction of the priest is in these verses. It is a prayer for the LORD to protect his people and give them prosperity. Blessed is the one who comes in the name of the LORD. The prophets Haggai and Zechariah revealed God's truth, and Zerubbabel completed God's plan for building the temple. The house of Israel had given God praise in his house. God is the LORD, the eternal one.

When Jesus made his triumphal entry into Jerusalem on the Sunday before his crucifixion, the people used words from this psalm to praise him. The people shouted, "Hosanna!" This is the Hebrew word for "Save now!" And they said, "Blessed is he who comes in the name of the LORD." (Matthew 21:9) They were looking for the Messiah who would overthrow the Romans. But he came to save them from their sins and give them eternal life by being their sacrifice nailed to a Roman cross. Blessed is Jesus Christ, who came in the name of the LORD. May we say, "You are my God, and I will praise you."

The psalm concludes with these words:

O give thanks to the LORD, for he is good!
For his mercy endures forever. 118:29

Psalm 119

God's Law is the Guide for our Life

The writer is unknown, but the psalm gives us some clues. The writer was a young man (verses 9 and 99) to whom God had made a "promise" (v. 123 ESV). But he was now suffering persecution (vv. 22, 23, 50, 51, 53, 61, 69, 71, 78, 84-87, 92, 95, 98, 110, 134, 139, 141, 143, 146, 150, 153, 157, 161, 174 and 176). Young David was anointed to be the next king of Israel, but he was being persecuted by king Saul and his followers. David may have written this psalm to remind himself that God's law was to be his guide for life. The psalm was too personal and too long to have been in the previous books of psalms. But when Ezra was collecting psalms for Book Five, he may have noticed that this psalm's teachings could be applied to the entire nation of Israel.

The blessings of God's law are declared in Psalm 119. God's law, his *torah,* includes all of his instructions and teachings. His law is also called his word, testimonies, statutes, commandments, precepts, ways, judgments and ordinances. Psalm 119 reminds us of Psalm 1:1-2, which says, "Blessed is the man who walks not in the counsel of the ungodly, nor stands in the way of sinners, nor sits in the seat of the scornful. But his delight is in the law of the LORD; and in his law he meditates day and night." This psalm is also like Psalm 19:7-11, written by David.

The psalm is divided into 22 stanzas that consist of eight verses. The Hebrew alphabet has 22 letters. All eight verses in the first stanza begin with the Hebrew letter Aleph; and all eight verses in the second stanza begin with Beth, and so on throughout the alphabet. This was to help the Hebrew reader in memorizing the psalm.

The words of this psalm need little comment.

Aleph
The Blessing of Obeying the Law of the LORD

Blessed are the undefiled in the way,
　who walk in the law of the LORD.
Blessed are they that keep his testimonies,
　and seek him with the whole heart.
They also do no iniquity; they walk in his ways.
Thou hast commanded us
　to keep your precepts diligently.
O that my ways were directed to keep your statutes!
Then I shall not be ashamed
　when I have respect unto all thy commandments.
I will praise thee with uprightness of heart,
　when I shall have learned thy righteous judgments.
I will keep thy statutes;
　O forsake me not utterly. 119:1-8

Beth
The Blessing of Cleansing by God's Word

How can a young man cleanse his way?
　By taking heed according to Your word.
With my whole heart I have sought You;
　Oh, let me not wander from Your commandments!
Your word I have hidden in my heart,
　that I might not sin against You.
Blessed are You, O LORD!
　Teach me Your statutes.
With my lips I have declared all the judgments
　of Your mouth.
I have rejoiced in the way of Your testimonies,
　as much as in all riches.
I will meditate on Your precepts,
　and contemplate Your ways.
I will delight myself in Your statutes;
　I will not forget Your word. 119:9-16 NKJV

Gimel
The Blessing of Guidance during Distress

Deal bountifully with your servant,
that I may live and keep your word.
Open my eyes that I may behold
wondrous things out of your law.
I am a sojourner on the earth;
hide not thy commandments from me!
My soul is consumed with longing
for your rules at all times.
You rebuke the insolent, accused ones,
who wander from your commandments.
Take away from me scorn and contempt,
for I have kept your testimonies.
Even though princes sit plotting against me,
Your servant will meditate on your statutes.
Your testimonies are my delight;
they are my counselors. 119:17-24 ESV

Daleth
The Way of Faithfulness and Life

My soul clings to the dusts;
Give me life according to your word.
When I told of my ways, you answered me;
teach me your statutes!
Make me understand the way of your precepts,
And I will meditate on your wondrous works.
My soul melts away for sorrow;
Strengthen me according to your word!
Put false ways far from me
And graciously teach me your law!
I have chosen the way of faithfulness;
I set your rules before me.
I cling to your testimonies, O LORD;
Let me not be put to shame!
I will run the way of your commandments
when you enlarge my heart. 119:25-32 ESV

He
Teach Me Your Way, O LORD

Teach me, O LORD, the way of Your statutes,
  and I shall keep it to the end.
Give me understanding, and I shall keep Your law;
  indeed, I shall observe it with my whole heart.
Make me walk in the path of Your commandments,
  for I delight in it.
Incline my heart to Your testimonies,
  and not to covetousness.
Turn away my eyes from looking at worthless things,
  and revive me in Your way.
Establish Your word to Your servant,
  who is devoted to fearing You.
Turn away my reproach which I dread,
  for Your judgments are good.
Behold, I long for Your precepts;
  revive me in Your righteousness. 119:33-40 NKJV

Waw
Give Me Your Mercies to Speak Your Word

Let thy mercies come also unto me, O LORD,
even thy salvation according to thy word.
So shall I have wherewith to answer him
who reproaches me, for I trust in thy word.
And take not the word of truth
  utterly out of my mouth,
  for I have hoped in thy judgments.
So I shall keep thy law continually forever and ever.
And I will walk at liberty;
  for I seek thy precepts.
I will speak of thy testimonies also before kings,
  and will not be ashamed.
And I will delight myself in thy commandments,
  which I have loved.
My hands also I will lift up to thy commandments;
  and I will meditate in thy statutes. 119:41-48

Zayin
Remembering God's Promises Gives Comfort

Remember your word to your servant,
    for you have given me hope.
My comfort in my suffering is this:
    Your promise preserves my life.
The arrogant mock me without restraint,
    but I do not turn from your law.
I remember your ancient laws, O LORD,
    and I find comfort in them.
Indignation grips me because of the wicked,
    who have forsaken your law.
Your decrees are the theme of my song
    wherever I lodge.
In the night I remember your name, O LORD,
    and I will keep your law.
This has been my practice:
    I obey your precepts. 119:49-56 NIV

Heth
God's Lovingkindness is My Portion

Thou art my portion, O LORD;
    I have said that I would keep thy words.
I entreated thy favor with my whole heart;
    be merciful to me according to thy word.
I thought on my ways,
    and turned my feet unto thy testimonies.
I made haste,
    and delayed not to keep thy commandments.
The bands of the wicked have robbed me;
    but I have not forgotten thy law.
At midnight I will rise to give thanks to thee
    because of thy righteous judgments.
I am a companion of all those who fear thee,
    and of those who keep thy precepts.
The earth, O LORD, is full of thy mercy;
    teach me thy statutes. 119:57-64

Teth
God Teaches through Afflictions

You have dealt well with thy servant, O LORD,
according to thy word.
Teach me good judgment and knowledge,
    for I have believed thy commandments.
Before I was afflicted, I went astray;
    but now I have kept thy word.
Thou art good, and do good; teach me thy statutes.
The proud have forged a lie against me;
    but I will keep thy precepts with my whole heart.
Their heart is as fat as grease;
    but I delight in thy law.
It is good for me that I have been afflicted;
    that I might learn thy statutes.
The law of thy mouth is better to me
    than thousands of gold and silver *pieces.*
        119:65-72

Yod
God's Hand of Providential Care

Thy hands have made me and fashioned me;
    give me understanding,
    that I may learn thy commandments.
They that fear thee will be glad when they see me,
    because I have hoped in thy word.
I know, O LORD, that thy judgments are right,
    and that thou in faithfulness have afflicted me.
Let, I pray thee, thy merciful kindness be for my
    comfort, according to thy word to thy servant.
Let thy tender mercies come to me that I may live,
    for thy law is my delight.
Let the proud be ashamed,
    for they dealt perversely with me without cause;
    but I will meditate in thy precepts.
Let those that fear thee turn to me,
    and those that have known thy testimonies.
Let my heart be sound in thy statutes;
    that I be not ashamed. **119:73-80**

Kaph
Hope in the Darkest Days

My soul faints with longing for your salvation,
  but I have put my hope in your word.
My eyes fail, looking for your promise;
  I say, "When will you comfort me?"
Though I am like a wineskin in the smoke,
  I do not forget your decrees.
How long must your servant wait?
  When will you punish my persecutors?
The arrogant dig pitfalls for me,
  contrary to your law.
All your commands are trustworthy;
  help me, for men persecute me without cause.
They almost wiped me from the earth,
  but I have not forsaken your precepts.
Preserve my life according to your love,
  And I will obey the statutes of your mouth. NIV
                                    119:81-88

Lamed
The Word of the LORD is Eternal

Your word, O LORD, is eternal;
  it stands firm in the heavens.
Your faithfulness continues through all generations;
  you established the earth, and it endures.
Your laws endure to this day,
  for all things serve you.
If your law had not been my delight,
  I would have perished in my afflictions.
I will never forget your precepts,
  for by them you have preserved my life.
Save me, for I am yours;
  I have sought out your precepts.
The wicked are waiting to destroy me,
  but I will ponder your statutes.
To all perfection I see a limit;
  But your commands are boundless. NIV **119:89-96**

Mem
Oh, How I Love God's Teachings!

Oh, how I love Thy law!
It is my meditation all the day.
Thy commandments make me wiser than
my enemies, for they are ever mine.
I have more insight than all my teachers,
for Thy testimonies are my meditation.
I understand more than the aged,
because I have observed Thy precepts.
I have restrained my feet from every evil way,
that I may keep Thy word.
I have not turned aside from Thine ordinances,
for Thou Thyself hast taught me.
How sweet are Thy words to my taste!
Yes, sweeter than honey to my mouth!
From Thy precepts I get understanding.
Therefore I hate every false way. 119:97-104 NASB

Nun
God's Word is a Light to My Path

Thy word is a lamp to my feet,
and a light to my path.
I have sworn, and I will confirm it,
that I will keep Thy righteous ordinances.
I am exceedingly afflicted.
Revive me, O LORD, according to your word.
O accept the freewill offerings of my mouth, O LORD,
and teach me Thine ordinances.
My life is continually in my hand,
yet I do not forget Thy law.
The wicked have laid a snare for me,
yet I have not gone astray from Thy precepts.
I have inherited Thy testimonies forever,
for they are the joy of my heart.
I have inclined my heart to perform Thy statutes
forever, even to the end. 119:105-112 NASB

Samek
God's Judgments upon the Double-minded

I hate the double-minded,
> but I love your law.
You are my hiding place and my shield;
> I hope in your word.
Depart from me, you evildoers,
> that I may keep the commandments of my God.
Uphold me according to your promise, that I may live,
> and let me not be put to shame in my hope!
Hold me up, that I may be safe
> and have regard for your statutes continually!
You spurn all who go astray from your statutes,
> for their cunning is in vain.
All the wicked of the earth you discard like dross,
> therefore I love your testimonies.
My flesh trembles for fear of you,
> and I am afraid of your judgments. 119:113-120 ᴱˢⱽ

Ayin
Looking for Salvation from the LORD

I have done what is just and right;
> do not leave me to my oppressors.
Give your servant a pledge of good;
> let not the insolent oppress me.
My eyes long for your salvation and
> for the fulfillment of your righteous promise.
Deal with your servant, give me understanding,
> that I may know your testimonies!
It is time for the LORD to act,
> for your law has been broken.
Therefore I love your commandments
> above gold, above fine gold.
Therefore I consider your precepts to be right;
> I hate every false way. 119:121-128 ᴱˢⱽ

Pe
God's Words Impart Understanding

Thy testimonies are wonderful;
  therefore my soul observes them.
The unfolding of Thy words gives light;
  it gives understanding to the simple.
I opened by mouth wide and panted,
  for I longed for Thy commandments.
Turn to me and be gracious to me,
  after Thy manner with those who love Thy name.
Establish my footsteps in Thy word,
  and do not let any iniquity have dominion over me.
Redeem me from the oppression of man,
  that I may keep Thy precepts.
Make Thy face shine upon Thy servant,
  and teach me Thy statutes.
My eyes shed streams of water,
  because they do not keep Thy law. 119:129-136 NASB

Tsadhe
God's Words are Righteous and Faithful

Righteous art thou, O LORD,
  and upright are thy judgments.
Thy testimonies that thou hast commanded are
  righteous and very faithful.
My zeal has consumed me,
  because my enemies have forgotten thy words.
Thy word is very pure; therefore, thy servant loves it.
I am small and despised;
  yet I do not forget thy precepts.
Thy righteousness is an everlasting righteousness,
  and thy law is the truth.
Trouble and anguish have taken hold on me;
  yet thy commandments are my delights.
The righteousness of thy testimonies is everlasting.
  Give me understanding, and I shall live.
119:137-144

Qoph

Prayers with Hope in God's Word

I cry out with my whole heart;
    Hear me, O LORD! I will keep Your statutes.
I cry out to You;
    Save me, and I will keep Your testimonies.
I rise before the dawning of the morning,
    And cry for help; I hope in Your word.
My eyes are awake through the night watches,
    That I may meditate on Your word.
Hear my voice according to Your lovingkindness;
    O LORD, revive me according to Your justice.
They draw near who follow after wickedness;
    They are far from Your law.
You are near, O LORD,
    And all Your commandments are truth.
Concerning Your testimonies, I have known of old
    that You have founded them forever. NKJV
                                        119:145-152

Resh

Revive Me according to Thy Word

Look upon my affliction and rescue me,
    for I do not forget Thy law.
Plead my cause and redeem me;
    Revive me according to Thy word.
Salvation is far from the wicked,
    for they do not seek Thy statutes.
Great are Thy mercies, O LORD;
    Revive me according to Thy ordinances.
Many are my persecutors and my adversaries,
    yet I do not turn aside from Thy testimonies.
I behold the treacherous and loathe them,
    because they do not keep Thy word.
Consider how I love Thy precepts; revive me,
    O LORD, according to Thy lovingkindness.
The sum of Thy word is truth, and everyone
    of Thy righteous ordinances is everlasting. NASB
                                        119:153-160

Shin

Loving God's Word Brings Peace

Princes persecute me without a cause,
   but my heart stands in of Your word.
I rejoice at Your word
   as one who finds a treasure.
I hate and abhor lying,
   but I love Your law.
Seven times a day I praise You,
   because of Your righteous judgments.
Great peace have those who love Your law,
   and nothing causes them to stumble.
LORD, I hope for Your salvation,
   and I do Your commandments.
My soul keeps Your testimonies,
   and I love them exceedingly.
I keep Your precepts and Your testimonies,
   for all my ways are before You. 119:161-168 NKJV

Tau

Let Me Live that I May Praise Thee

Let my cry come near before thee, O LORD;
   give me understanding according to thy word.
Let my supplication come before thee;
   deliver me according to thy word.
My lips shall utter praise,
   when thou hast taught me thy statutes.
My tongue shall speak of thy word;
   for all thy commandments are righteousness.
Let thine hand help me;
   for I have chosen thy precepts.
I have longed for thy salvation, O LORD,
   and thy law is my delight.
Let my soul live, and it shall praise thee;
   and let thy judgments help me.
I have gone astray like a lost sheep; seek thy servant;
   for I do not forget thy commandments.
                              119:169-176

Psalm 120
A Song of Ascents

A Cry for Delivance from the Deceitful

This is the first in a series of psalms, 120 to 134, which are called "A Song of Ascents." These fifteen psalms were used for going up to Jerusalem for the feast days. (Deut. 16:16) [10] Verse five says, "I dwell in Meshech … among the tents of Kedar." NKJV The war-loving people of Meshech and Kedar lived a great distance apart. This is figurative language for the Samaritans and Ammonites. (Read Ezra 4-6.)

> **In my distress I cried to the LORD,**
> **and He heard me.**
> **Deliver my soul, O LORD, from lying lips**
> **and from a deceitful tongue.**
> **What shall be given to you,**
> **or what shall be done to you, you false tongue?**
> **Sharp arrows of the warrior,**
> **With coals of the broom tree!**
>
> **Woe is me, that I dwell in Meshech,**
> **That I dwell among the tents of Kedar!**
> **My soul has dwelt too long with one who hates peace.**
> **I am for peace;**
> **But when I speak, they are for war. 120:1-7** NKJV

As the Jews went up to Jerusalem to worship in the temple, they were reminded that the temple was built because the LORD had answered their prayers.

God's spiritual temple, the church, is being constructed of spiritual stones, Christians. (1 Peter 2:1-5) Unbelievers have spoken lies and deceitful words in order to stop the building of this temple. This has been true since the first century. (Acts 28:17-22; 1 Cor. 3:16)

---

[10] James Limburg, *Psalms,* p. 420

Psalm 121
A Song of Ascents

Help from the LORD

As they approach Jerusalem, the worshipers will see the hills surrounding the city and ask, "Where does my help come from?" And then they will answer, "My help comes from the LORD, the Maker of heaven and earth." This psalm tells of God's providential care for his people.

> I lift up my eyes to the hills—
> where does my help come from?
> My help comes from the LORD,
> the Maker of heaven and earth.
>
> He will not let your foot slip—
> he who watches over you will not slumber;
> indeed, he who watches over Israel
> will neither slumber nor sleep.
>
> The LORD watches over you—
> the LORD is your shade at your right hand;
> the sun will not harm you by day,
> nor the moon by night.
> The LORD will keep you from all harm—
> He will watch over your life;
> the LORD will watch over your coming and going
> both now and forevermore. 121:1-8 NIV

In the New Testament, Paul assures Christians, "And we know that God causes all things to work together for good to those who love God, to those who are called according to His purpose." NASB (Romans 8:28) God can even turn our troubles and hardships into something good; he has a purpose for them. (2 Cor. 12:7-9)

Psalm 122
A Song of Ascents, of David

Peace & Joy in the House of the LORD

The house of the LORD was the tabernacle that David had erected when he brought the Ark of the Covenant to Jerusalem. (2 Sam. 6:17) David expresses his joy when he went there to worship the LORD. The house of God and the throne of David were in Jerusalem. So, David urges the people to "pray for the peace of Jerusalem." This would be the prayer and joy of those who would worship the LORD in the restored city and temple after the exile.

I was glad when they said to me,
　"Let us go into the house of the LORD."
Our feet shall stand within thy gates, O Jerusalem!
Jerusalem is built as a city that is compact together,
　　where the tribes go up, the tribes of the LORD,
　　unto the testimony of Israel,
　　to give thanks to the name of the LORD.
For there are set thrones of judgment,
　　the thrones of the house of David.
Pray for the peace of Jerusalem;
　　they shall prosper that love thee.
Peace be within thy walls,
　　And prosperity within thy palaces.
For my brethren and companions' sake,
　　I will now say, "Peace be within thee."
Because of the house of the LORD our God,
　　I will seek thy good. 122:1-9

For Christians, "the house of God is the church of the living God." (1 Timothy 3:15) "And let us consider one another to stir up love and good works, not forsaking the assembling of ourselves together." NKJV (Heb. 10:24-25) The church is "the heavenly Jerusalem." (Heb. 12:22-23; Galatians 4:22-26; Rev. 21) We enjoy peace in the church of Christ.

Psalm 123
A Song of Ascents

A Prayer for Mercy

As the worshipers approached the temple in Jerusalem, they acknowledged their need for God's mercy. The Samaritans were showing contempt and hostility toward them. The Jews looked up to heaven and prayed for the LORD to have mercy upon them. They were God's slaves who were dependent upon him for their well-being.

> **I lift up my eyes to you,**
> **to you whose throne is in heaven.**
> **As the eyes of slaves look to the hand of their master,**
> **As the eyes of a maid look to the hand of her mistress,**
> **So our eyes look to the LORD our God,**
> **till he shows us his mercy.**
>
> **Have mercy on us, O LORD, have mercy on us,**
> **for we have endured much contempt.**
> **We have endured much ridicule from the proud,**
> **much contempt from the arrogant. 123:1-4** NIV

Christians are called **"slaves of righteousness"** in Romans 6:16-18. NASB Those of the world call Christians "goodie goods" and "narrow-minded bigots." Ridicule and contempt are poured out upon Christians today by the secular humanists. But we know our need for God's mercy because of our own imperfections. We also need his mercy to give us strength to be faithful as his slaves in the midst of the world's opposition. His word instructs us, *"Do not love the world, nor the things in the world. If any one loves the world, the love of the Father is not in him. For all that is in the world, the lust of the flesh, the lust of the eyes and the boastful pride of life, is not from the Father, but is from the world. And the world is passing away, and also its lusts; but the one who does the will of God abides forever."* NASB (1 John 2:15-17)

Psalm 124
A Song of Ascents, of David

Having the LORD on Our Side

Having the LORD on Israel's side had saved the nation from annihilation more than once. David's army of Israel was greatly outnumbered by the armies of Syria and Ammon, but God gave the victory to David and Israel. (2 Sam. 10) In the days of King Hezekiah, things looked hopeless when the Assyrians destroyed all of Israel and besieged Jerusalem; but God destroyed the entire Assyrian army in one night. (2 Kings 18 & 19:) When the Babylonians destroyed all the cities of Judah, including Jerusalem and the temple, it looked like Israel had been completely annihilated. But the LORD stirred up the spirit of Cyrus king of Persia to restore the nation of Israel in Jerusalem by rebuilding the temple of the LORD. (Ezra 1) As the Jews went up to Jerusalem to worship, they sang: "If it had not been the LORD who was on our side."

If it had not been the LORD who was on our side,
**   now may Israel say:**
"If it had not been the LORD who was on our side,
**   when men rose up against us,**
Then they had swallowed us up alive,
**   when their wrath was kindled against us;**
Then the waters had overwhelmed us,
**   the stream had gone over our soul;**
Then the proud waters had gone over our soul."

Blessed be the LORD,
**   who has not given us as a prey to their teeth.**
Our soul has escaped as a bird
**   out of the snare of the fowlers;**
The snare is broken and we have escaped.
Our help is in the name of the LORD,
**   who made heaven and earth. 124:1-8**

Psalm 125

A Song of Ascents

The LORD Surrounds His People

**Those who trust in the LORD are as Mount Zion,
which cannot be moved, but abides forever. 124:1** NASB

As worshipers approached Mount Zion and the temple, they were reminded of their need to have confidence in the LORD. The temple representing God's presence had been rebuilt on Mount Zion. "Zion became a general name for the whole city of Jerusalem." [11] Those who trust in the LORD will live forever in heavenly Mount Zion, singing praises before the throne of God forever. (Revelation 14:1-5; 21:5-8; 22:1-5; Hebrews 3:6)

**As the mountains surround Jerusalem,
So the LORD surrounds His people
From this time forth and forever. 125:2** NASB

Jerusalem, which is on a mountain, is surrounded by mountains. The Mount of Olives is on the east; separated from Jerusalem by the Valley of Kidron. The Valley of Hinnom is on the south and west of Jerusalem.[12] There were mountains south, west and north of Jerusalem.

The LORD surrounds and protects his people as the mountains that surround Jerusalem. God's people are called the heavenly Jerusalem in Hebrews 12:22-23 and in Revelation 21. Christians have God's protection and his love.

**For the scepter of wickedness shall not rest
on the land allotted to the righteous,
Lest the righteous reach out their hands to iniquity.
125:3** NKJV

---

[11] F. N. Peloubet, *Peloubet's Bible Dictionary,* p. 307
[12] George E. Wright, *The Westminster Historical Atlas to the Bible,* p. 109

Although wickedness may rule for a while in the land of God's people, it will not continue, lest the righteous become wicked themselves. *"God is faithful, who will not allow you to be tempted beyond what you are able, but with the temptation will also make the way of escape that you may be able to bear it."* ^{NKJV} (I Cor. 10:13) That is why God punished his people with invading armies from time to time, and then delivered them; and righteousness was restored in their land.

> **Do good, O LORD, to those that are good,**
> **And to those that are upright in their hearts.**
> **As for such as turn aside to their crooked ways,**
> **the LORD shall lead them forth**
> **with the workers of iniquity;**
> **But peace shall be upon Israel. 125:4-5**

The way of escape in the time of temptation is to remember that only the LORD has the power to bless and to curse forever. Israel now refers to those who have "power with God" because they have been redeemed by the blood of Jesus Christ. (Gal. 6:14-16; Rom. 2:28-29)

Psalm 126
A Song of Ascents

Sowing in Tears; Reaping in Joy

During their years in foreign lands, the people of Israel were sowing in tears. Now, they were reaping in joy.

> **When the LORD turned again the captivity of Zion,**
> **we were like those who dream.**
> **Then was our mouth filled with laughter,**
> **and our tongue with singing.**
> **Then they said among the heathen,**
> **"The LORD has done great things for them."**
> **The LORD has done great things for us;**
> **whereof we are glad. 126:1-3**

The decree of Cyrus king of Persia allowed those of Israel to return to Jerusalem and rebuild the temple of the LORD. This was like a dream; it seemed too good to be true. (Acts 12:9) But God had caused their deliverance from captivity. (Ezra 1:1-40) Even the nations were impressed what the LORD had done for his people Israel.

God has freed Christians, who were once captives of sin. (Romans 6:16-18) We should be telling others about the great things our Lord has done for us. (Mark 5:19) Others will notice the changes for good in our lives. We have something to sing about – a new life that is eternal!

Bring back our captivity, O LORD,
As the streams in the South. 126:4 NKJV

Zerubbabel led 42,360 Jews back to Jerusalem from Babylon in 536 BC. (Ezra 2) However, many more Jews were still in exile. Seventy-eight years later, Ezra led a second group of Jews back to Jerusalem in 458 BC. Nehemiah led a third group from Babylon to Jerusalem in 445 BC. The Israelites who had been conquered by the Assyrians were also allowed to return by the decree of Cyrus. The return of the people of Israel from captivity is compared to the streams of water that flowed into the dry water-beds in southern Palestine after the rains.

They that sow in tears shall reap in joy.
He who goes forth and weeps,
   bearing precious seed,
Shall doubtless come again rejoicing,
   bringing in the sheaves with him. 126:5-6

Those who sow the precious seed in tears shall reap in joy when the harvest comes. What is **the precious seed**? Jesus said that the **seed** of the kingdom of God "is the **word** of God." (Luke 8:1,11) A Christian has been "born again" of **seed** that is "incorruptible, by the **word** of God, which lives and abides forever." (1 Peter 1:23)

When David was king over all of Israel, God said to him, "I will set up your seed after you, who will come from your body, and I will establish his kingdom. Your house and your kingdom shall be established forever before you." ^{NKJV}(2 Samuel 7:12,16) Before the Jews went into exile in Babylon, God told them by his prophet Habakkuk, "The just shall live by his faith." (Hab. 2:4) "So then, **faith** come by hearing, and hearing **by the word of God**." (Romans 10:17)

While captives in foreign lands, the faithful continued teaching the word of God and living by faith. They were sowing in tears the precious seed. That is the reason they returned to Jerusalem when given the opportunity.

After the Jews returned to Jerusalem, there would be times when they would have to sow God's word in tears. When they laid the foundation of the new temple, the Samaritans brought them trouble for several years. But the Jews reaped in joy when the temple was completed. Many years later when Nehemiah was rebuilding the walls of Jerusalem, he was opposed by the Samaritans. However, the Jews were filled with joy when the walls were completed.

Christians will sow the word of God with tears because of the opposition from unbelievers. When Christ returns, those who are faithful will reap in joy with all those who are saved. The night before his death on the cross, Jesus told his disciples, "These things I have spoken to you that in me you might have peace. In the world, you shall have tribulation; but be of good cheer, I have overcome the world." (John 16:33)

Let's remember Psalm 126 when we sing the gospel songs: *The Heart Shall Reap in Joy* and *Bringing in the Sheaves.*

Psalm 127

A Song of Ascent of Solomon

Prosperity from the LORD

This psalm by Solomon is very much like his proverbs. He tells us that man's prosperity comes from the LORD. The Jews, having returned to Jerusalem from exile, needed to be reminded of their dependence upon God's blessings for their success. The temple was to be built— also their houses, their families, their businesses and their farms. They needed a time of peace along with materials, tools, skill, wisdom, good health and strength.

> **Unless the LORD builds the house,**
> **They labor in vain who build it;**
> **Unless the LORD guards the city,**
> **The watchman keeps awake in vain.**
> **It is vain for you to rise up early, to retire late,**
> **To eat the bread of painful labors;**
> **For He gives to His beloved even in his sleep.** NASB
> **127:1-2**

A man rises early in the morning and works hard for success until late at night; but if he has not sought help from God, his labors will be worthless. Jesus asked, "For what is a man profited if he shall gain the whole world and lose his own soul?" (Matthew 16:26)

> **Lo, children are a heritage of the LORD;**
> **and the fruit of the womb is a reward.**
> **As arrows are in the hand of a mighty man,**
> **so are the children of the youth.**
> **Happy is the man that has his quiver full of them;**
> **they shall not be ashamed,**
> **But they speak with the enemies in the gate. 127:3-5**

God rewards us with godly children. Each one is a precious gift. The children of our youth will protect us from harm when we grow old.

Psalm 128

A Song of Ascents

The Family that Fears the LORD

To fear the LORD means to respect and love the LORD like a child toward his parents. If we fear God, we will trust in his truth and great power, and we will want to live the way he tells us to live. "The fear of the LORD is the beginning of knowledge." (Proverbs 1:7)

> **Blessed is everyone who fears the LORD,**
>   **who walks in his ways!**
> **You shall eat the fruit of the labor of your hands;**
>   **you shall be blessed, and it shall be well with you.**
>   **128:1-2** ESV

Solomon, being guided by the Holy Spirit in his search for happiness, said: "Let us hear the conclusion of the whole matter: "Fear God, and keep his commandments." (Eccl. 12:13) Earlier he had said, "It is good and proper for a man to eat and drink, and to find satisfaction in his toilsome labor under the sun during the few days of life God has given him." NIV (Eccl. 5:18) Some godly men and women, who have feared the LORD, have suffered as martyrs. The Bible tells us, "Godliness is profitable unto all things, having the promise of the life that now is, and of that which is to come." (1 Tim. 4:8)

> **Your wife will be like a fruitful vine**
>   **within your house;**
> **your children will be like olive shoots**
>   **around your table.**
> **Behold, thus shall the man be blessed**
>   **who fears the LORD. 128:3-4** ESV

A godly wife is the heart of the family. She is like a fruitful vine. Children who gather around a table to eat are like olive branches, symbolizing peace and joy.

> **The LORD shall bless you from Zion!**
> **May you see the prosperity of Jerusalem**
> **all the days of your life!**
> **May you see your children's children!**
> **Peace be upon Israel! 128:5-6** ^{ESV}

The Jews would praise God in his temple, thanking him for his blessings and praying for continued prosperity. The temple in Jerusalem was destroyed by the Romans in AD 70. However, God is still on his holy throne in heaven. (Rev. 14:1-3; 22:1-5) As Christians, we are "the Israel of God." (Galatians 6:15-16) Let us pray to the LORD for our peace and prosperity. May we live to see our grandchildren!

Psalm 129
A Song of Ascents

Victory over Israel's Enemies

This psalm portrays the history of the nation of Israel as a person, as in Hosea 11.

> **Many a time they have afflicted me from my youth.**
> **May Israel now say:**
> **Many a time they have afflicted me from my youth;**
> **Yet they have not prevailed against me. 129:1-2**

As a young nation, Israel suffered slavery to the Egyptians. The LORD gave Israel a homeland in Canaan. We read in The Book of Judges that Israel was oppressed by the Mesopotamians, the Moabites, the Philistines, the Canaanites, the Midianites, the Amalekites and the Ammonites. Later, the Assyrians conquered the northern tribes of Israel and carried them away to other countries. Then, the Babylonians destroyed Jerusalem and the temple, and the Jews lived in exile for many years. However, the Persians conquered the Babylonians and permitted the Jews to return to Jerusalem and rebuild the temple of the LORD. The nation of Israel was restored!

Plowmen have plowed my back
    and made their furrows long.
But the LORD is righteous;
    he has cut me free from the cords of the wicked.
                          129:3-4 ^{NIV}

Figurative language is used to describe their suffering. The scars on the back of a slave from a master's whip were like long furrows made by a plowman. Also, this may be a description of the complete destruction of a city. But the righteous LORD had set his nation of Israel free!

The Samaritans had hindered the building of the temple and the restoration of Jerusalem. So, the psalm concludes with a prayer that those who hate Zion will not be successful in their efforts.

May all who hate Zion,
    be put to shame and turned backward,
Let them be like the grass upon the housetops,
    which withers before it grows up;
With which the reaper does not fill his hand,
    or the binder of sheaves his bosom;
Nor do those who pass by say,
    "The blessing of the LORD be upon you;
    We bless you in the name of the LORD." ^{NASB}
                          129:5-8

Psalm 130
A Song of Ascents

The LORD Redeems Israel

The nation of Israel had been afflicted and conquered by other nations. This was due to the sins of its people. Joseph's brothers sold him to be a slave in Egypt; in time, their descendants became slaves to the Egyptians. Because the people of Israel disobeyed God's commandments and worshiped idols, God allowed them to be oppressed and conquered by other nations.

After ten thousand Jews were taken captive to Babylon, the prophet Jeremiah wrote these words from Jerusalem:

"For thus says the LORD: 'After seventy years are accomplished at Babylon, I will visit you and perform my good word toward you in causing you to return to this place. .... You shall seek Me and find Me, when you search for Me with all your heart. ... I will gather you from all the nations and from all the places where I have driven you, says the LORD, and I will bring you again into the place where I caused you to be carried away captive.'" (Jer. 29:10-14)

Psalm 130 seems to have been written by a devout Jew during the exile in Babylon. He was praying to the LORD as he had been instructed to do. (Read Daniel 9:1-19)

> **Out of the depths I have cried out unto thee, O LORD.**
> **Lord, hear my voice!**
> **Let thine ears be attentive to**
> **the voice of my supplications. 130:1-2**

Out of great distress and afflictions, the writer of the psalm prays aloud to *Yahweh*—the self-existing, eternal One. God is also called *Adonai,* the powerful Ruler.

> **If thou, LORD, should mark iniquities,**
> **O Lord, who shall stand?**
> **But there is forgiveness with thee,**
> **that thou may be feared. 130:3-4**

If the Lord should hold all of our sins against us, no one would be able to stand before him. We may approach God because he has provided the way of forgiveness. "For all have sinned and come short of the glory of God." (Rom. 3:23) "For the wages of sin is death; but the gift of God is eternal life through Jesus Christ." (Rom. 6:23) "The Lord is not willing that any should perish, but that all should come to repentance." (2 Peter 3:9; also read Romans 2:4)

I wait for the LORD, my soul waits;
   and in his word, I do hope.
My soul waits for the Lord
   more than they that watch for the morning;
I say, more than they that watch for the morning.
                                        130:5-6

This Jew who was praying for deliverance from exile in Babylon was like a night watchman looking forward to his relief from guard duty at dawn. He has faith and hope because God had promised that the day would come when the people of Israel would be restored to their homeland.

Jesus has promised a gathering of his followers to an even brighter future. He has said to them, "Do not let your hearts be troubled. Trust in God; trust also in me. In my father's house are many rooms; if it were not so, I would have told you. I am going there to prepare a place for you. And if I go and prepare a place for you, I will come back and take you to be with me that you also may be where I am." NIV (John 14:1-3)

Let Israel hope in the LORD!
For with the LORD there is mercy,
And with him is plenteous redemption.
And he shall redeem Israel from all his iniquities.
                                        130:7-8

As the travelers journeyed to the rebuilt temple in Jerusalem, they are reminded of how the LORD had delivered them from the depths of their sufferings. Their homeland had been destroyed, and they had been exiles in foreign lands. These afflictions were because of their sins. But God in his mercy had forgiven them and redeemed them from all their sins. He had restored them to their homeland to worship him in his temple. They could expect future blessings from the LORD. May we also **hope in the LORD!** "We have this hope as an anchor for the soul, firm and secure." NIV (Hebrews 6:19)

Psalm 131

A Song of Ascents of David

Hope in God Brings Contentment

This psalm of David prepared the hearts of those going to Zion to worship the LORD. It confesses the humility and contentment of a person whose hope is in the LORD.

> LORD, my heart is not haughty,
> nor my eyes lofty;
> Neither do I exercise myself in great matters,
> or in things too high for me.
> Surely I have behaved and quieted myself,
> as a child that is weaned of his mother;
> My soul is even as a weaned child.
> Let Israel hope in the LORD
> from henceforth and forever. 131:1-3

Psalm 132

A Song of Ascents

God's Dwelling Place in Zion

The worshipers were ascending Mount Zion, because the LORD had chosen Zion for his habitation. (v. 13) The Most Holy Place represented the presence of the LORD. Behind the veil was The Ark of the Covenant, containing the two stone tablets on which the Ten Commandments were written. The Ark is called "the footstool of our God" in 1 Chronicles 28:2.

The tabernacle was erected at Mount Sinai as Israel began its journey to the promised land of Canaan. It was made "according to the pattern" that was shown to Moses. (Hebrews 8:5) Israel was instructed to worship "where the LORD your God chooses, out of all your tribes, to put His name for His dwelling place, and there you shall go." (Deuteronomy 12:5)

During the conquest of Canaan, the tabernacle was at Gilgal near the Jordan River. (Joshua 4:19, 5:10) Then the tabernacle was set up at Shiloh, and it remained there during the period of the Judges. But when Eli was the high priest, his two sons desecrated the tabernacle. (1 Samuel 3:22) They also took the Ark with them to fight against the Philistines hoping that it would give them the victory. But the Ark was captured, and "the glory of God" was departed from the tabernacle. (1 Samuel 4:21-22)

The Philistines took the Ark to the house of their god Dagon in Ashdod. But in the morning, they found Dagon fallen on its face before the Ark of the LORD. The next day they found Dagon again fallen before the Ark. This time, the head of Dagon and its hands were broken off. And the LORD struck the people of Ashdod with a plague. Then the Ark was taken to Gath and to Ekron, and their people also suffered with tumors from the LORD. (1 Samuel 5)

The Philistines put the Ark on a cart drawn by two milk cows, which had young calves that were taken away. This was a test to see if the LORD had brought these disasters upon Dagon and the Philistines. "Then the cows headed straight for the road to Beth Shemesh (in Israel), lowing as they went, and did not turn aside." (1 Samuel 6:8-12) The Ark was then taken to Kirjath-Jearim. Twenty years later, Samuel led Israel in battle against the Philistines, and God gave Israel the victory. (1 Samuel 7:1-13)

The Ark was placed in a tent in a field on a hill that belonged to Abinadab, who was a Levite. Kirjah-Jearim, meaning "the city of forests," was about eight miles NW of Jerusalem. God was directing the destiny of the Ark of the Covenant. The Ark remained at Kirjah-Jearim until the reign of David, whose great desire was to bring it to Jerusalem. David could not truly rest until he had brought the Ark to Jerusalem; and he made preparations for his son Solomon to build the temple on Mount Zion.

LORD, remember David and all his afflictions:
How he swore to the LORD,
    and vowed to the mighty God of Jacob:
I will not go into the tabernacle of my house,
    nor go up into my bed;
I will not give sleep to my eyes
    or slumber to my eyelids,
Until I find out a place for the LORD,
    a habitation for the mighty God of Jacob.
Lo, we heard of it at Ephrathah;
    we found it in the fields of the wood.
We will go into his tabernacles;
    we will worship at his footstool.
Arise, O LORD, into thy rest.
    You and the ark of thy strength.
Let thy priests be clothed with righteousness;
    and let thy saints shout for joy.
For thy servant David's sake,
    turn not away the face of thy anointed.
                  132:1-10

God responded to David's vows with an oath of his own in the remaining verses of Psalm 132.

The LORD has sworn in truth to David;
He will not turn from it:
    Of the fruit of thy body, I will set up thy throne.
If thy children will keep my covenant
    and my testimonies that I shall teach them,
Their children shall also sit upon thy throne
    forevermore. **132:11-12**

God made this promise to David when David stated his desire to build a temple for the LORD. (2 Samuel 7:1-17)

For the LORD has chosen Zion;
He has desired it for his habitation.
This is my rest forever.
Here I will dwell for I have desired it.
              132:13-14

When Solomon dedicated the temple, he said: "I have built a house for the name of the LORD God of Israel. And I set there a place for the ark, wherein is the covenant of the LORD." (1 Kings 8:20-21) He asked, "But will God indeed dwell on the earth? Behold, the heaven and heaven of heavens cannot contain thee; how much less this house that I have built?" (1 Kings 8:27) The temple on Mount Zion in Jerusalem was foreshadowing the true dwelling place of God on heavenly Mount Zion. (Gal. 4:22-31; Heb. 12:22; Rev. 14:1-3) The redeemed are the new, holy Jerusalem. (Rev. 21:1-10)

> **"I will abundantly bless her with provision;**
> **I will satisfy the poor with bread.**
> **I will also clothe her priests with salvation,**
> **And her saints shall shout aloud for joy.**
> **There I will make the horn of David grow;**
> **I will prepare a lamp for My Anointed.**
> **His enemies I will clothe with shame,**
> **But upon Himself, His crown shall flourish."** NKJV
> **132:15-18**

The ultimate Seed of David is Christ Jesus our Lord; and the ultimate blessing is heaven. "They shall hunger no more, neither thirst anymore." (Rev. 7:16-17)

In the new covenant of Christ, all Christians are priests, and they are clothed with Christ's righteousness and his salvation. (1 Peter 2:9; Galatians 3:26-29) They are joyful saints, because they have been set apart for God's service.

The Lord God gave to Jesus "the throne of his father David, and of his kingdom there will be no end." (Luke 1:31-33) The Hebrew word *Messiah* is translated **Anointed** in verse 17. Christ is the Greek word for anointed, and He is "the light of the world." (John 8:12; 14:6)

Psalms 133

A Song of Ascents of David

The Blessing of Unity

Behold! How good and how pleasant it is
    for brethren to dwell together in unity! 133:1
It is like the precious oil upon the head,
Running down on the beard, the beard of Aaron,
Running down on the edge of his garments.
It is like the dew of Hermon,
    descending upon the mountains of Zion;
For there the LORD commanded the blessing—
    Life forevermore. 133:1-3 NKJV

As David saw those of Israel ascending Mount Zion to worship the LORD, he said, "Look!" He was pleased to see those of God's family being together in unity as they assembled for one of the annual feasts. (Deut. 16)

Moses poured some anointing oil on Aaron's head to consecrate him to serve as priest. (Lev. 8:12) This oil had a fragrant aroma. (Exodus 30:22-25)

Unity is refreshing as the morning dew, which gives life to the grass and plants. And from heavenly Zion, God gives eternal life. (Rev. 21:4-6; 14:1-3)

Jesus prayed that all of his followers would be united. He said, "That they all may be one; as thou Father, are in me, and I in thee, that they also may be one in us, that the world may believe that thou hast sent me." (John 17:21)

Hebrews 10:23-25 exhorts Christians, "Let us hold fast the confession of our hope without wavering, for He who promised is faithful. And let us consider one another in order to stir up love and good works, not forsaking the assembling of ourselves together." NKJV We need to keep the unity of the Spirit in the bond of peace. (Eph. 4:3)

Psalm 134

A Song of Ascents

Praising the LORD in His Temple

Praise the LORD, all you servants of the LORD
who minister by night in the house of the LORD.
Lift up your hands in the sanctuary and praise
the LORD.

May the LORD, the Maker of heaven and earth,
bless you from Zion. 134:1-3 NIV

This is the last psalm of the Songs of Ascents, which began with Psalm 120. The worshipers are now in the temple calling for the priests to lead them in praises to be made to the LORD. The priests pray that the Maker of heaven and earth would bless them.

Psalm 135

Praising the Greatness of the LORD

This psalm is an example of the praises given to the LORD in his temple. He is praised for his greatness.

Praise ye the LORD!
Praise ye the name of the LORD!
Praise him, O ye servants of the LORD!
Ye that stand in the house of the LORD,
in the courts of the house of our God.
Praise the LORD, for the LORD is good;
Sing praises to his name, for it is pleasant.
For the LORD has chosen Jacob unto Himself,
And Israel for his peculiar treasure. 135:1-4

The LORD is to be praised because his name is *Yahweh,* I AM, the self-existing eternal One. (Exodus 3:13-14; John 8:58) Everyone is to praise the LORD, including those in the courts of the temple. He is to be praised because He is good. (Matthew 19:17) God had chosen the descendants of Jacob, the nation of Israel, for himself to be his own special treasured possession. Those who are a new creation in Christ are "the Israel of God" today. (Galatians 15-16; 2 Corinthians 5:17; 1 Peter 2:9)

> For I know that the LORD is great,
>   and that our Lord is above all gods.
> Whatever the LORD pleased
>   that He did in heaven and in the earth,
>   in the seas and all deep places.
> He causes the vapors to ascend
>   from the ends of the earth;
> He makes lightnings for the rain;
> He brings the wind out of his treasures. 135:5-7

The LORD is great! He rules with authority over heaven and earth. He controls the weather! He causes water to evaporate and ascend into the sky and become clouds. He makes lightnings, rain and wind. He has used weather conditions to cause men to consider their ways. (Read Haggai 1:7-11)

> He smote the first-born of Egypt,
> Both of man and beast.
> He sent signs and wonders into your midst, O Egypt,
> Upon Pharaoh and all his servants.
> He smote many nations,
> And slew mighty kings,
>   Sihon, king of the Amorites,
>   And Og, king of Bashan,
>   And all the kingdoms of Canaan;
> And He gave their land as a heritage,
> A heritage to Israel His people.
> Thy name, O LORD, is everlasting,
> Thy remembrance, O LORD, throughout
>   all generations.
> For the LORD will judge His people,
> And will have compassion on His servants. NASB
>   135:8-14

The greatness of the LORD may be seen in history as his prophets correctly predicted the rise and fall of nations. The LORD by his prophet Isaiah predicted, 150 years in advance, that Cyrus king of Persia would defeat Babylon and restore Jerusalem in Isaiah 44:28 through 45:4. Daniel predicted the coming of Alexander the Great. (Daniel 8) The LORD causes the rise and fall of nations, according to Jeremiah 18:5-10. The LORD is our Judge.

> **The idols of the heathen are silver and gold,**
> > **the work of men's hands.**
> **They have mouths, but they speak not;**
> **They have eyes, but they see not;**
> **They have ears, but they hear not;**
> **Neither is there any breath in their mouths.**
> **They that make them are like unto them;**
> **So is everyone who trusts in them. 135:15-18**

In contrast to our Almighty God, idols are powerless. All of God's people should praise the LORD!

> **Bless the LORD, O house of Israel!**
> **Bless the LORD, O house of Aaron!**
> **Bless the LORD, O house of Levi!**
> **Ye that fear the LORD, bless the LORD!**
> **Blessed be the LORD out of Zion,**
> > **who dwells at Jerusalem!**
> **Praise ye the LORD! 135:19-21**

Psalm 136

The LORD's Mercy Endures Forever

Each verse of this psalm ends with the words: "for his mercy endures forever." We are to give thanks to the LORD for his divine goodness, authority, wisdom and creative power in verses 1-9. In verses 10-26, thanks are to be given to Him for delivering Israel from bondage in Egypt and giving them the land of Canaan as a heritage.

O give thanks to the LORD, for he is good!
    For his mercy endures forever.
O give thanks to the God of gods!
    For his mercy endures forever.
O give thanks to the Lord of lords!
    For his mercy endures forever.
To Him who alone does great wonders,
    For his mercy endures forever.
To Him that by wisdom made the heavens,
    For his mercy endures forever.
To Him who stretched out the earth above the waters,
    For his mercy endures forever.
To Him who made great lights,
    For his mercy endures forever.
The sun to rule the day,
    For his mercy endures forever.
The moon and stars to rule the night,
    For his mercy endures forever. 136:1-9

To Him who smote Egypt in their firstborn,
    For his mercy endures forever.
And brought out Israel from among them,
    For his mercy endures forever.
With a strong hand, and with an outstretched arm,
    For his mercy endures forever.
To Him who divided the Red Sea into parts,
    For his mercy endures forever.
And made Israel to pass through the midst of it,
    For his mercy endures forever.
But overthrew Pharaoh and his host in the Red Sea,
    For his mercy endures forever.
To Him who led his people through the wilderness,
    For his mercy endures forever.
To Him who smote great kings,
    For his mercy endures forever.
And slew famous kings,
    For his mercy endures forever:
Sihon king of the Amorites,
    For his mercy endures forever.

And Og the king of Bashan,
  For his mercy endures forever.
And gave their land for a heritage,
  For his mercy endures forever.
Even a heritage to Israel his servant,
  For his mercy endures forever.
Who remembered us in our low estate,
  For his mercy endures forever.
And has redeemed us from our enemies,
  For his mercy endures forever.
Who gives food to all flesh,
  For his mercy endures forever.
O give thanks to the God of heaven,
  For his mercy endures forever. **136:10-26**

Psalm 137

Remembering Zion while in Babylon

This psalm expresses the emotions and the thoughts of the Jews while in Babylon after the destruction of the temple and the city of Jerusalem.

By the rivers of Babylon, there we sat down,
  yea, we wept,
  when we remembered Zion.
We hung our harps upon the willows
  in the midst thereof. **137:1-2**

The main rivers of Babylon were the Tigris and Euphrates, and from them flowed many water courses. Ezekiel was among the Jewish captives by the river Chebar. (Ezekiel 1:1) The Jews often gathered by the rivers to pray. (Acts 16:13) They remembered going to Zion playing harps as they sang joyful songs to the Lord; but now the city of Jerusalem and the temple were in ruins. So, they sat down and wept. They could not sing anymore. Figuratively, they had hung their harps on the willow trees that grew alongside the river.

For there they that carried us away captive
    required of us a song;
And they that wasted us
    required of us mirth, saying,
"Sing us one of the songs of Zion."

How shall we sing the LORD's song in a strange land?
                                                137:3-4

The Babylonians may have wanted to cheer up the Jews by singing joyful songs from their past. The Jews asked, "How can we be joyful? How can we forget the LORD's temple that was in Zion?" They were in a foreign land, but they would not forget Jerusalem!

If I forget you, O Jerusalem,
    let my right hand forget its skill!
If I do not remember you,
    let my tongue cling to the roof of my mouth—
If I do not exalt Jerusalem above my chief joy. NKJV
                                                137:5-6

The Jew in captivity was saying, "If I forget Jerusalem, may I lose my ability to play the harp and to sing songs." Learning of God and worshiping him in Jerusalem was his greatest joy. We need to ask, "What is my chief joy?"

Remember, O LORD,
    what the Edomites did on the day Jerusalem fell.
"Tear it down," they cried,
    "tear it down to its foundations!" 137:7 NIV

God did remember what Edom did. (Jeremiah 49:7-21; Obadiah 1-4, 10-14) The prophecy of Obadiah 7 was fulfilled when Nabonidus king of Babylon invaded Edom.

O daughter of Babylon, doomed to destruction,
    happy is he who repays you
    for what you have done to us—
he who seizes your infants and dashes them
    against the rocks." 137:8-9 NIV

The LORD had predicted the destruction of Babylon in Isaiah 13:17-22. The killing of infants and children was a common wartime practice. (2 Kings 8:12; Nahum 3:10) The prayer of the Jews in captivity was for God to do what he had said he would do. "Vengeance is Mine," says the LORD. (Deut. 32:35)

Psalm 138
A Psalm of David

The LORD Regards the Lowly

This is the first of eight psalms in the final collection of David's psalms (138-145). The setting seems to be when the LORD promised David that he would establish the throne of his kingdom forever. (2 Samuel 7:4-16) When the angel Gabriel announced the birth of Jesus Christ to Mary, he referred to this promise. (Luke 1:26-33, 46-52)

> **I praise Thee with my whole heart;**
> > **before the gods I will sing praise unto thee;**
> **I worship toward thy holy temple,**
> > **and praise thy name for thy lovingkindness**
> > **and for thy truth,**
> > **for thou hast magnified thy word**
> > **above thy name.**
> **In the day when I cried, you answered me;**
> > **And strengthened me with strength in my soul.**
> > > **138:1-3**

David took the city of Jerusalem and made it his city soon after his being made king of Israel. (2 Sam. 5:4-7) When the Philistine kings came to dethrone him, David prayed to the LORD, who answered his prayer by giving him the strength to defeat his enemies. (2 Sam. 5:17-25)

After these victories, God promised to establish David's throne forever. (2 Sam. 7:1, 12-13, 16) This caused David to ask, "Who am I, O Lord GOD? And what is my family?

Thou art great, O LORD God; for there is none like thee! And what one nation in the earth is like thy people, even Israel, which you redeemed to you from Egypt, from the nations and their gods?" (2 Sam. 7:18-23) David offered his prayer of thanksgiving to the only true God—the omnipotent LORD, who had made these great promises to one who had been a lowly shepherd boy. (2 Sam. 7:8) The "temple" in verse two refers to tabernacle for the Ark of the Covenant that was in Jerusalem. (2 Sam. 6:17) David thanked the LORD for his steadfast love and faithfulness.

> **All the kings of the earth shall praise thee, O LORD,**
> **When they hear the words of thy mouth.**
> **Yea, they shall sing in the ways of the LORD,**
> **For great is the glory of the LORD.**
> **Though the LORD is high,**
> **Yet he has respect for the lowly;**
> **But the proud he knows afar off. 138:4-6**

"And men came from all peoples to hear the wisdom of Solomon, from **all the kings of the earth** who had heard of his wisdom." NASB (1 Kings 4:34) God gave Solomon his wisdom—words from God's mouth. (1 Kings 4:29) The glory of Solomon was the glory of the LORD.

When God chose the virgin Mary to be the mother of Jesus, she said, "He has regarded the low estate of his handmaiden." (Luke 1:48) He is mindful of the humble, and he exalts them. (James 4:10; 1 Peter 5:6) He gives comfort and strength to them. (Isaiah 40:29) The LORD also knows the thoughts and acts of the proud. But they are not close to God; he resists them. (1 Peter 5:5)

> **Though I walk in the midst of trouble,**
> **You will revive me;**
> **You shall stretch forth your hand against**
> **the wrath of my enemies,**
> **And your right hand shall save me. 138:7**

David remembered the many times God had revived him during the years that Saul was seeking to kill him. In the future, David would trust in God to deliver him when the great armies of Ammon and Syria came against Israel (2 Sam. 10) David trusted in the LORD when his own son Absalom rebelled against him. (2 Sam. 15)

> **The LORD will perfect that which concerns me;**
> **Thy mercy, O LORD, endures forever.**
> **Forsake not the works of thine own hands. 138:8**

David believed the LORD would keep his promise. For over six hundred years after the destruction of Jerusalem in 586 BC, no one of David's dynasty was on the throne.

On the Day of Pentecost after the resurrection of Jesus from the dead, the fulfillment of God's promise to David was made known. Peter declared, "Men and brethren, let me speak freely to you of the patriarch David. … God had sworn with an oath to him that of the fruit of his body, according to the flesh, He would raise up the Christ to sit of his throne, … (He) spoke concerning the resurrection of the Christ." Peter then quoted Psalm 110:1, "The LORD said to my Lord, 'Sit thou on my right hand, until I make thy foes thy footstool.'" Peter concluded, "Therefore, let all the house of Israel know assuredly that God has made this Jesus, whom ye crucified, both Lord and Christ." (Acts 2:29-36) And the words were fulfilled that were spoken to Mary by the angel Gabriel concerning the birth of her son, "The Lord God shall give to him the throne of his father David, and he shall reign over the house of Jacob forever, and of his kingdom there shall be no end." (Luke 1:32-33) Jesus invites the lowly to come to him. (Matthew 11:28-29)

The Hebrew word *hesed* is used twice in this psalm. In verse two it is God's **lovingkindness**. In verse eight, it is God's enduring **mercy**.

Psalm 139

A Psalm of David

God's Knowledge of Each Person

God has a personal interest in each one of us. The divine attributes of the LORD are revealed in this psalm.

> O LORD, you have searched me
> and you know me.
> You know when I sit down and when I rise;
> you perceive my thoughts from afar.
> You discern my going out and my lying down;
> you are familiar with all my ways.
> Before a word is on my tongue
> You know it completely, O LORD. 139:1-4 ^{NIV}

These verses tell us of the **omniscience** of God. He knows all things. He knows us as individual persons. He knows all of our thoughts, our words and our actions. We cannot conceal anything from God.

> Thou hast beset me behind and before,
> and laid thine hand upon me.
> Such knowledge is too high,
> I cannot attain unto it. 139:5-6

These verses reveal God's **providential care** for us as individuals. David felt his closeness to God. (Psalm 23) It is hard for us to comprehend the greatness of God's care for us each day.

> Where can I go from Thy Spirit?
> Or where can I flee from Thy presence?
> If I ascend to heaven, Thou art there;
> If I make my bed in Sheol, behold, Thou art there.
> If I take the wings of dawn,
> If I dwell in the remotest part of the sea,
> Even there Thy hand will lead me.
> And Thy right hand will lay hold of me.
> 139:7-10 ^{NASB}

These verses describe the **omnipresence** of God. He is everywhere. The LORD says, "Heaven is My throne, and the earth is My footstool." (Isaiah 66:1) Sheol is the place for departed spirits—the dead. Regardless of how high or low a person may go; God will be there. It does not matter how far east or west he might travel; he cannot flee from God. Jonah learned this lesson the hard way. (Jonah 1-2) God's presence is a blessing to the godly.

> **If I say, "Surely the darkness shall cover me,"**
> **even the night shall be light about me.**
> **Yes, the darkness hides not from thee;**
> **but the night shines as the day.**
> **The darkness and the light are both alike**
> **to thee. 139:11-12**

No one is able to hide in the dark from God. "Nothing in all creation is hidden from God's sight. Everything is uncovered and laid bare before the eyes of him to whom we must give account." ᴺᴵⱽ (Hebrews 4:13) The LORD sees all things in the dark as well as the light.

> **For you created my inmost being;**
> **you knit me together in my mother's womb.**
> **I praise you because I am fearfully and**
> **wonderfully made;**
> **your works are wonderful,**
> **I know that full well.**
> **My frame was not hidden from you**
> **when I was made in the secret place.**
> **When I was woven together in the depths**
> **of the earth,**
> **your eyes saw my unformed body.**
> **All the days ordained for me**
> **were written in your book**
> **before one of them came to be. 139:13-16** ᴺᴵⱽ

Theses verses praise God for his **omnipotence** (his great creative power) and for his **foreknowledge**. Our highly complex human body was formed in our mother's womb. A small egg from our mother was fertilized by one tiny sperm from our father. Truly, we are indeed fearfully and wonderfully made.

The book that has **"all the days ordained for me"** may refer to our chromosomes. "Human beings typically have 46 chromosomes in most of their cells. Chromosomes are made up largely of DNA and proteins. DNA is the coded information for the passing of characteristics from parents to offspring. Chromosomes consist of large numbers of DNA units called *genes*." [13] The color of our hair, eyes, skin, and many other things (including our health) were determined even before we were born.

> **How precious also are thy thoughts to me, O God!**
> **How great is the sum of them!**
> **If I should count them,**
> **they are more in number than the sand;**
> **When I awake, I am still with thee. 139:17-18**

God's thoughts produce his wonderful works. And God said, "Let us make man in our image, according to our likeness." (Genesis 1:26) David could see God's care for him throughout his life, even from his conception. God's thoughts were precious to him. We also should treasure God's thoughts for us. Brother L. O. Sanderson wrote the hymn, "The Lord Has Been Mindful of Me." The chorus says, "He blesses and blesses again!" We should be able to see God's providential care for us, even in difficult times. (Philippians 4:10-13; James 1:2-4; Eph. 1:17-18) God was with David at all times of the night and the day.

> **Surely you will slay the wicked, O God;**
> **Depart from me therefore, ye bloody men.**
> **For they speak against Thee wickedly,**
> **And your enemies take thy name in vain. 119:19-20**

---

[13] J. Herbert Taylor, *The World Book Encyclopedia,* Vol. 3, p. 418

David did not want to associate with God's enemies, who spoke against the LORD and took his name in vain. In the New Testament, the apostle Paul wrote, "Be ye not unequally yoked together with unbelievers; for what fellowship has righteousness with unrighteousness? ... Come out from among them, and be separate, says the LORD ... and I will receive you." (2 Corinthians 6:14-17)

> **Do not I hate them, O LORD, that hate Thee?**
> **And am I not grieved with those that**
> **rise up against thee?**
> **I hate them with a perfect hatred;**
> **I count them my enemies. 139:21-22**

There is "a godly jealousy." (2 Cor. 11:1) And there is "a perfect hatred." (Psalm 139:22) "Hate the evil, and love the good." (Amos 5:15) "Through thy precepts I get understanding; therefore, I hate every false way." (Psalm 119:104) David hated those who hated God. God's enemies would be David's enemies. David was grieved with the ungodly. God is also grieved with the ungodly. "But they rebelled and grieved His Holy Spirit." NASB (Isaiah 63:10) Jesus also was "grieved" for the hardness of men's hearts. (Mark 3:5) Jesus said, "He that is not with me is against me." (Matthew 12:30) Are we with God? David is saying I'm with the LORD.

> **Search me, O God, and know my heart;**
> **Try me, and know my thoughts;**
> **And see if there be any wicked way in me,**
> **And lead me in the way everlasting. 139:23-24**

David concludes with a prayer for God to know his heart and his thoughts. He wants to repent of any wicked way that God may find. He needs God's forgiveness. He wants to be led in the way of everlasting life with God in heaven. "And I will dwell in the house of the LORD forever." (Psalm 23:6) This should also be our prayer to God.

Psalm 140

A Psalm of David

Prayer for Deliverance from Evil Men

This psalm is similar to Psalm 52, which was written when Saul's servant Doeg falsely accused the high priest Ahimelech of conspiring with David to kill king Saul. It describes "evil" and "violent men" who "sharpen their tongue like a serpent." King Saul ordered Doeg to kill Ahimelech and all eighty-five priests at Nob. Saul's servants killed both men and women and also children and babies in the city of Nob, the home of the priests. (1 Sam. 22:8-20) David prays for deliverance from these evil men. Paul quotes verse 3 in Romans 3:13.

> Deliver me, O LORD, from evil men;
> Preserve me from violent men,
> Who plan evil things in their hearts;
> They continually gather for war.
> They sharpen their tongues like serpents;
> The poison of asps is under their lips. Selah
>
> Keep me, O LORD, from the hands of the wicked;
> Preserve me from violent men,
> Who have purposed to make my feet stumble.
> The proud have hidden a snare for me, and cords;
> They have spread a net by the wayside;
> They have set traps for me. Selah. 140:1-5 NKJV

David did not want to kill Saul. (1 Samuel 24:1-20) He prayed for God's protection from Saul's men who were seeking to kill him. He prayed in faith because God had anointed him to be the next king of Israel. Christians should pray for protection from Satan's snares to entrap us in sin. Jesus taught his disciples to pray, "And lead us not into temptation, but deliver us from evil." (Matt. 6:13) We can pray with faith in God's promises. (2 Peter 1:11) Each temptation is a test of one's faith. (1 Peter 1:5-7)

I said to the LORD, "Thou art my God;
Hear the voice of my supplication, O LORD.
O GOD the Lord, the strength of my salvation,
You have covered my head in the day of battle.
Do not grant, O LORD, the desires of the wicked;
Do not further his wicked device;
Lest they exalt themselves." Selah 140:6-8

God was David's helmet to protect his head in the time of battle. We have "the helmet of salvation" as part of God's armor to protect us. (Ephesians 6:11-17)

"As for the head of those who surround me,
Let the evil of their lips cover them;
Let burning coals fall upon them;
Let them be cast into the fire,
Into deep pits, that they rise not up again.
Let not a slanderer be established in the earth;
Let evil hunt the violent man to overthrow him."
140:9-11 NKJV

These verses are imprecatory—calling for God to curse the wicked. The LORD had said, "Vengeance is Mine, ... For the day of their calamity is near, ... For the LORD will vindicate His people." (Deut. 32:35-36) In Romans 12:19, Christians are reminded of this promise. Time after time, God delivered David from his enemies. Saul suffered a humiliating defeat in his final battle with the Philistines. Three of his sons were killed, and Saul was severely wounded. He ended his life by falling upon his own sword. (1 Samuel 31:1-4)

I know the LORD will maintain the cause of the afflicted
and the right of the poor.
Surely the righteous shall give thanks unto thy name;
the upright shall dwell in thy presence. 141:12-13

The LORD promises, "He who overcomes shall inherit all things; and I will be his God, and he shall be my son." (Revelation 21:7)

Psalm 141
A Psalm of David

A Prayer for Guidance to Do Right

We must guard what we say and do, especially while we are being mistreated. David wrote this psalm when he was being persecuted, either by Saul or by his own son, Absalom.

> **LORD, I cry unto Thee, make haste unto me!**
> **Give ear unto my voice, when I cry unto Thee.**
> **Let my prayer be set forth before Thee as incense;**
> **And the lifting up of my hands as the evening sacrifice.**
> **141:1-2**

David is in great danger! He is threatened by violent enemies. So, he prays with his hands lifted up toward heaven for God to act quickly. Incense is associated with prayers in Revelation 5:8. The evening offering of incense was an hour of prayer. (Acts 3:1; Luke 1:10) "And the smoke of the incense, which came with the prayers of the saints, ascended up before God." (Rev. 8:4)

> **Set a watch, O LORD, before my mouth;**
> **keep the door of my lips.**
> **Incline not my heart to any evil thing,**
> **to practice wicked works with men**
> **that work iniquity;**
> **And let me not eat of their dainties. 141:3-4**

David wanted to say and do right. The word of the LORD is a **guard** over what we say, think and do. Psalm 119 tells us we can keep our way pure by taking heed to God's word and by seeking God with our whole heart. David said, "Your word I have hidden in my heart that I might not sin against Thee." (Psalm 119:9-11) When we are tempted, God guards our heart by helping us to remember his word. Jesus overcame temptations by quoting God's word. (Matthew 4:3-11) David did not desire sin's riches.

Let the righteous smite me in kindness and reprove me;
 it is oil for my head;
Do not let my head refuse it,
For still my prayer is against their evil deeds.
Their judges are thrown down by the sides of the rock,
And they hear my words, for they are pleasant.
As when one plows and breaks open the earth,
Our bones have been scattered at the mouth of Sheol.
 141:5-7 NASB

David would gladly accept the discipline and rebuke of a righteous person; it would be refreshing as excellent oil that is poured upon the head of a welcomed guest. Jesus said, "It is the Spirit who gives life; the flesh profits nothing. The words that I speak to you are spirit, and they are life. (John 6:63) David prays that the wicked will learn that his words were true, because they were the LORD's words. (2 Peter 1:1; Acts 2:29-30) As plowed ground is open to receive the seed, may we open our hearts to receive God's word. We should pray that sinners will learn that God's words are true before they die.

But my eyes are upon You, O GOD the Lord;
In You I take refuge;
Do not leave my soul destitute.
Keep me from the snares they have laid for me.
And from the traps of the workers of iniquity.
Let the wicked fall into their own nets,
While I escape safely. 141:8-10 NKJV

David was looking to God for his defense and safety. He prays for deliverance from his enemies' snares and traps—both physical and spiritual. He does not want to become like his enemies, repaying evil with evil. His enemies would be destroyed by their own wicked ways. Later, Solomon wrote: "Do not say, 'I'll pay you back for this wrong!' Wait for the LORD, and he will deliver you." NIV (Proverbs 20:22)

Psalm 142
Maskil of David, when he was in the cave.

A Prayer of One Feeling Alone

This instructional psalm of David is telling us how he felt when he first fled from Saul. He went to the Philistine city of Gath and received no help. (1 Samuel 21:10-15) Then David went to the cave of Adullam, where he was hiding alone before his family and many others came to him in answer to this prayer. (1 Samuel 22:1-2)

I cry aloud to the LORD;
　I lift up my voice to the LORD for mercy.
I pour out my complaint before him;
　before him I tell my trouble.

When my spirit grows faint within me,
　it is you who know my way.
In the path where I walk
　men have hidden a snare for me.
Look to my right and see;
　no one is concerned for me;
I have no refuge;
　no one cares for my life.

I cry to you, O LORD;
　I say, "You are my refuge,
　my portion in the land of the living."
Listen to my cry,
　for I am in desperate need;
rescue me from those who pursue me,
　for they are too strong for me.
Set me free from my prison,
　that I may praise your name.
Then the righteous will gather about me,
　because of your goodness to me. **142:1-7** NIV

About four hundred righteous supporters came to him. When we are feeling alone, mistreated and forsaken, let's remember Psalm 142 and Hebrews 13:5-6.

Psalm 143
A Psalm of David

A Prayer for Guidance

Absalom's rebellion in 2 Samuel 15-18 seems to be the setting. Although David's sin with Bathsheba had been forgiven, he was suffering the consequences that God had predicted. (2 Sam. 7:9-11) David shows his repentance and his desire for God's guidance. This is the last of the seven psalms that describe true repentance; they are Psalms 6, 32, 38, 51, 102, 130 and 143.

> **Hear my prayer, O LORD,**
> **give ear to my supplications;**
> **In thy faithfulness answer me,**
> ***and* in thy righteousness.**
> **And enter not into judgment with thy servant,**
> **For in thy sight no man living shall be justified.**
> **143:1-2**

David is praying for mercy, because God is faithful to keep his promises. (2 Sam. 7:12-17) God's righteousness includes his holy nature, his love and mercy, as well as his justice for those who reject him.

David did not desire absolute justice, but God's mercy. "By the deeds of the law there shall no flesh be justified in his sight ... For all have sinned and come short of the glory of God." (Romans 3:20, 23) Confessing his sins and his need of mercy, David is God's servant. We should not serve the LORD to earn his blessings, but we should serve him because of his mercy and forgiveness. (Rom. 6:1-6)

> **For the enemy has persecuted my soul;**
> **he has smitten my life down to the ground.**
> **He has made me to dwell in darkness**
> **as those who have been long dead.**
> **Therefore, my spirit is overwhelmed within me;**
> **my heart within me is desolate. 143:3-4**

Satan was **the enemy** that was causing the rebellion led by Absalom. We also are warned, "Your **enemy** the devil prowls around like a roaring lion looking for someone to devour." ^{NIV} (1 Peter 5:8) David was suffering the results of his own sins. His own son was rebelling against him! He felt crushed to the ground like those in the darkness of death. His spirit faints with defeat at the overpowering conditions. All comfort was gone.

> **I remember the days of old;**
> **I meditate on all thy works;**
> **I muse on the work of thy hands.**
> **I stretch forth my hands unto thee;**
> **My soul *thirsts* after thee, as a thirsty land. Selah.**
> **143:5-6**

David remembered when he was just a shepherd boy. God helped him to kill a lion and a bear. (1 Sam. 17:34-36) Then God gave him victories over the giant Goliath and over all of Israel's enemies. David also focused his thoughts on all of God's works: his creation, the flood, his saving Noah's family, his making those of Abraham, Isaac and Jacob his chosen family, the Exodus, the conquest of Canaan and God's promise to establish David's throne forever. (2 Samuel 7) David took in these thoughts of God's power. It changed his thinking. He stretched out his hands toward God and prayed. He confessed that his soul was needing God as a dry land needs water.

> **Hear me speedily, O LORD;**
> **My spirit fails!**
> **Hide not thy face from me,**
> **Lest I be like those who go down into the pit.**
> **Cause me to hear thy lovingkindness in the morning;**
> **For in thee do I trust;**
> **Cause me to know the way wherein I should walk;**
> **For I lift up my soul unto thee. 143:7-8**

David needed an answer from the LORD soon, because his own power was fading away. He needed God's help— his steadfast love and mercy early in the morning. David was putting his trust and hope in the LORD. We also need to put our trust in God—not in ourselves and other men. David prayed for guidance: **"Cause me to know the way wherein I should walk.** This should also be our prayer.

God has revealed to us the way in which we should walk. The New Testament of Christ is the gift of the Holy Spirit. **"His divine power has given unto us all things that pertain unto life and godliness."** NASB (2 Peter 1:3) Jesus had promised his apostles, **"The Holy Spirit**, whom the Father will send in My name, He **will teach you all things,** and bring to your remembrance all that I said to you." (John 14:26) The Holy Spirit revealed the new covenant by inspiring the apostles and the first century prophets, whose teachings were confirmed by miracles. (Ephesians 3:1-7; Hebrews 2:1-4) That mission of the Holy Spirit has been accomplished! The New Testament tells us the way we should live. Let's read and obey it.

> **Deliver me from my enemies, O LORD!**
> **I have fled to you for refuge!**
> **Teach me to do your will,**
> **for you are my God!**
> **Let your good Spirit lead me on level ground!**
>
> **For your name's sake, O LORD, preserve my life!**
> **In your righteousness bring my soul out of trouble!**
> **And in your steadfast love you will cut off my enemies,**
> **and you will destroy all the adversaries of my soul,**
> **for I am your servant. 143:9-12** ESV

David asks the LORD to deliver him from his enemies, to teach him to do God's will, to let his Spirit safely lead him and preserve his life. David was confident in God's righteousness—not in his own. He was God's servant.

Psalm 144
A Psalm of David

The LORD is Our Protector and Provider

Blessed be the LORD my Rock,
Who trains my hands for war,
And my fingers for battle—
My lovingkindness and my fortress,
My shield and *the One* in whom I take refuge,
Who subdues my people under me. 144:1-2 NKJV

David praises the LORD for giving him the strength and skill to overcome his enemies. God was his protector. This seems to have been written after Absalom's death and David's restoration to the throne. (2 Samuel 18 – 19) Compare this psalm with Psalm 18, which David wrote after God had delivered him from king Saul.

LORD, what is man that You take knowledge of him?
Or the son of man, that You are mindful of him?
Man is like a breath:
His days are like a passing shadow. 144:3-4 NKJV

Why does God take notice of lowly man? Why does he protect us and provide for us? Man is insignificant when compared with God's vast creation of the universe. Verse three repeats the thoughts of Psalm 8:4. Our life on earth is like a breath; it passes away so quickly, like a shadow when the sun goes down.

Bow down thy heavens, O LORD, and come down;
Touch the mountains, and they shall smoke.
Cast forth lightning, and scattering them;
Shoot out thine arrows, and destroy them.
Send thine hand from above;
Rid me and deliver me out of great waters,
From the hand of strange children,
Whose mouth speaks vanity, and their right hand is
a right hand of falsehood. 144:5-8

David is figuratively describing how God had delivered him from Absalom's rebellion. Mountains in poetry are used to represent kingdoms. "The Most High rules in the kingdom of men." (Daniel 4:17, 25)

> **I will sing a new song to you, O God;**
>> **on the ten-stringed lyre I will make music to you,**
> **to the One who gives victory to kings,**
>> **who delivers his servant David from**
>> **the deadly sword. 144:9-10** ^{NIV}

David is singing to God a new song of salvation! In the past, David had been threatened with death many times, but the LORD had always delivered him. And now, God had given to him another victory!

> **Deliver me and rescue me**
>> **from the hands of foreigners**
> **whose mouths are full of lies,**
>> **whose right hands are deceitful.**
>
> **Then our sons in their youth**
>> **will be like well-nurtured plants,**
> **and our daughters will be like pillars**
>> **carved to adorn a palace.**
> **Our barns will be filled**
>> **with every kind of provision,**
> **Our sheep will increase by the thousands,**
>> **by tens of thousands in our fields;**
>> **our oxen will draw heavy loads.**
> **There will be no breaches of wall,**
>> **no going into captivity,**
>> **no cry of distress in our streets.**
>
> **Blessed are the people of whom this is true;**
>> **Blessed are the people whose God is the LORD.**
>>>> **144:11-15** ^{NIV}

David prays for the LORD's protection and his providing needed blessings for his people in the future. When Israel turned to idols, the nation lost its protection and blessings.

Psalm 145
David's Psalm of Praise

The LORD is Great and Good

David says, "Great is the LORD." (v. 3) and "The LORD is good." (v. 9) He praises God for his wondrous works and his compassionate mercy and goodness. "The LORD is righteous in all his ways." (v. 17) David's last psalm is one of praise to God.

> **I will extol thee, my God, O King;**
> **and I will bless thy name forever and ever.**
> **Every day I will bless thee;**
> **and I will praise thy name forever and ever.**
> **Great is the LORD,**
> **and greatly to be praised;**
> **And his greatness is unsearchable. 145:1-3**

King David recognized God as his King. "The LORD has established his throne in heaven, and his kingdom rules over all." (Psalm 103:19) David continues to praise God's name forever through his psalms. God's greatness is not fully known to us due to our human limitations.

> **One generation shall praise thy works to another,**
> **And shall declare thy mighty acts.**
> **I will speak of the glorious honor of thy majesty,**
> **And of thy wondrous works.**
> **And men shall speak of the might of thy terrible acts;**
> **And I will declare thy greatness.**
> **They shall abundantly utter the memory of**
> **thy great goodness,**
> **And shall sing of thy righteousness. 145:4-7**

The praise of God's greatness and goodness is to be passed on from generation to generation. This is primarily the duty of parents. Hezekiah prayed, "It is the living who give thanks to Thee, as I do today. A father tells his sons about Thy faithfulness." [NASB] (Is. 38:19)   The LORD says,

"And these words, which I command you this day shall be in your heart. And you shall teach them diligently to your children." (Deut. 6:6-7) Each generation needs to know about God's power—the creation, the great flood that destroyed all mankind except for Noah and his family, the ten plagues upon Egypt, the destruction of the Egyptian army in the Red Sea, the fall of the walls of Jericho, the conquest of Canaan and other "terrible acts" which produce the fear and reverence of God. "Behold therefore the goodness and severity of God: on those who fell, severity; but toward you, goodness, if you continue in His goodness. Otherwise, you also will be cut off." (Romans 11:22) God's great power and goodness are like an ever-flowing fountain. God alone is totally good and righteous. (Matthew 20:17)

> The LORD is gracious and full of compassion,
> Slow to anger and of great mercy.
> The LORD is good to all,
> And his tender mercies are over all his works. 145:8-9

God came down on Mount Sinai and proclaimed to Moses that he is "The LORD God, merciful and gracious, longsuffering, and abundant in goodness and truth." (Exodus 34:1-6) But he will punish those who break his covenant. (Exodus 34:7-16) **The LORD is good to all.** "He makes his sun to rise on the evil and on the good, and sends rain on the just and on the unjust." (Matthew 5:45) "The LORD is ... not willing that any should perish, but that all should come to repentance." (2 Peter 3:9)

> All thy works shall praise thee, O LORD;
>   and thy saints shall bless thee.
> They shall speak of the glory of thy kingdom,
>   and talk of thy power,
> To make known to the sons of men his mighty acts,
>   and the glorious majesty of his kingdom. 145:10-12

"The heavens declare the glory of God." (Psalm 19:1) The redeemed shall praise God for the gift of his Son, our Savior. (John 3:16) They will tell others of God's eternal kingdom. (2:44; Luke 1:31-33; Acts 2:29-36; Rev. 11:15)

Thy kingdom is an everlasting kingdom,
And thy dominion endures throughout all generations.
145:13

When Solomon was made king of Israel, the Bible says, "Then Solomon sat on **the throne of the LORD as king.**" (1 Chronicles 29:22) The kingdom of Israel was actually the kingdom of God. In the new covenant, the redeemed are brought into the kingdom of Christ. (Col. 1:12-14) Christians are now God's "holy nation." (1 Peter 2:9-10) God is the supreme ruler throughout all time and forever.

The LORD upholds all who fall,
And raises up all who are bowed down.
The eyes of all look expectantly to You;
And You give them their food in due season.
You open Your hand
And satisfy the desires of every living thing.
145:14-16 NKJV

The LORD has power and mercy to lift up all who fall and feel depressed. Jesus says, "Come unto me, all ye who labor and are heavy laden, and I will give you rest." (Matthew 11:28) God provides food for mankind and for every animal, fish and bird! "Your heavenly Father knows that you have need of all these things. But seek first the kingdom of God and his righteousness; and all these things shall be added unto you." (Matthew 6:32-33) Children are taught to pray, "God is great. God is good. Let us thank him for our food."

The LORD is righteous in all his ways,
and holy in all his works.
The LORD is near to all those who call upon him
in truth.

> He will fulfill the desire of those who fear him;
> He also will hear their cry, and save them.
> The LORD preserves all those who love him:
> But all the wicked he will destroy. 145:17-20

The LORD is righteous in his laws and in his providential care of us and his creation. But most of all, he is righteous in his saving us eternally through the blood of Jesus Christ, his dear Son. His righteousness includes his justice and his mercy. Grace and truth go together in John 1:14 and 17. God hears the prayers of those who sincerely and truly seek him. He fulfills the desires of those who love and respect him. But he will destroy all the wicked. "Let us have grace, whereby we may serve God acceptably with reverence and godly fear." (Hebrews 12:28) We have been saved to serve God—not sin. (Romans 6:1-18)

> My mouth shall speak the praise of the LORD;
> And let all flesh bless his holy name forever and ever.
> 145:21

David praises the LORD, and he encourages all human beings to praise God's holy name (his eternal goodness and great power) forever. The book of Psalms concludes with five psalms that begin with the same command: "Praise ye the LORD."

Psalm 146

Praise the LORD for Our Hope

"Blessed is he ... whose hope is in the LORD." (v.5) When we trust in men, they may disappoint us. But we can be assured and glad when we trust in the LORD, who made heaven and earth. (v. 6) We are to praise the LORD. "The LORD reigns forever!" (v. 10)

Praise the LORD.

Praise the LORD, O my soul.
I will praise the LORD all my life;
I will sing praise to my God as long as I live.

Do not put your trust in princes,
    in mortal men, who cannot save.
When their spirit departs, they return to the ground;
    on that very day their plans come to nothing.

Blessed is he whose help is the God of Jacob,
    whose hope is in the LORD his God,
the Maker of heaven and earth, the sea,
    and everything in them—
    the LORD, who remains faithful forever.
He upholds the cause of the oppressed and
    gives food to the hungry.
The LORD sets prisoners free,
    the LORD gives sight to the blind,
The LORD lifts those who are bowed down,
    the LORD loves the righteous.
The LORD watches over alien and sustains
        the fatherless and widow,
    but he frustrates the ways of the wicked.

The LORD reigns forever,
    your God, O Zion, for all generations.

Praise the LORD! NIV

Psalm 147

Blessings to Restored Israel

This psalm praises the LORD for restoring the nation of Israel to their homeland and rebuilding Jerusalem after being scattered by the Assyrians and Babylonians. "The Most High is sovereign over the kingdoms of men and gives them to anyone he wishes." ^NIV (Daniel 4:17)

> **Praise ye the LORD!**
> **For it is good to sing praises unto our God;**
> **For it is pleasant, and praise is comely.**
> **The LORD builds up Jerusalem;**
> **He gathers together the outcasts of Israel.**
> **He heals the broken in heart,**
> **And binds up their wounds.**
> **He tells the number of the stars;**
> **He calls them all by their names.**
> **Great is our Lord, and of great power;**
> **His understanding is infinite.**
> **The LORD lifts up the meek;**
> **He casts the wicked down to the ground. 147:1-6**

Singing praises to the LORD is enjoyable. It is fitting and proper for us to praise him. He builds, gathers, heals and binds up our wounds. Our God is great!

His knowledge of all things is infinite. Only God can count the stars of heaven, and he knows each star by name. God said Abraham's descendants would be many as the stars of heaven (Genesis 15:5), and "those who are of faith are sons of Abraham." ^NKJV (Galatians 3:7, 26-29) God knows all of his children by name. (John 10:3) The LORD has the power to lift up the humble and to cast down the wicked and proud.

Sing unto the LORD with thanksgiving.
Sing praise upon the harp unto our God,
Who covers the heaven with clouds,
Who prepares rain for the earth,
Who makes grass to grow upon the mountains.
He gives to the beasts his food,
And to the young ravens which cry. 147:7-9

Paul reminds us, "The living God made the heaven, the earth, the sea, and all things that are in them. He did good, gave us rain from heaven and fruitful seasons, filling our hearts with food and gladness." ^{NKJV} (Acts 14:15-17) God has provided for all our needs. He is in control of the weather to bless us and to punish us. He may call "for a drought" because of our disobedience. (Haggai 1:11)

He does not delight in the strength of the horse;
He takes no pleasure in the legs of man.
The LORD takes pleasure in those who fear him,
In those who hope in his mercy. ^{NKJV} **147:10-11**

God delights more in those who fear him and seek his mercy than he does in the physical strength and beauty of the horse or that of man. Mankind often delights more in God's creation than in God. Paul writes in Romans 1:25, they "worshiped and served the creature rather than the Creator."

Praise the LORD, O Jerusalem;
Praise thy God, O Zion!
For he has strengthened the bars of thy gates;
He has blessed thy children within thee.
He makes peace in thy borders,
And fills thee with the finest of the wheat. 147:12-14

This psalm may have been written for the dedication of the walls of Jerusalem by Nehemiah. (Neh. 12:27-31) They now were enjoying peace and prosperity; they were no longer troubled by the Samaritans. (Neh. 8:10)

> He sends his commandment to the earth;
>> his word runs very swiftly.
> He spreads the snow like wool
>> and scatters the frost like ashes.
> He hurls down his hail like pebbles.
>> Who can withstand his icy blast?
> He sends his word and melts them;
>> He stirs up his breezes, and the waters flow. ^{NIV}
>> 147:15-18

God's word controls the weather. "The word of God" sent the great flood in the days of Noah. (2 Peter 3:5-7) After the flood, God promised, "While the earth remains, seedtime and harvest, cold and heat, and summer and winter, day and night shall not cease." (Genesis 8:22) At the LORD's command he sends snow that covers and beautifies the earth with a garment of white. He sends cold and hot weather.

> He shows his word to Jacob,
>> his statutes and his judgments to Israel.
> He has not dealt so with any nation;
> And as for his judgments,
>> they have not known them.
>
> Praise ye the LORD! 147:19-20

"The law was given by Moses, but grace and truth came by Jesus Christ." (John 1:17) "His divine power has granted to us everything pertaining to life and godliness through the true knowledge of Him who called us by His own glory and excellence." ^{NASB} (2 Peter 1:3) The Bible was revealed to us through the nation of Israel. It is the gift of the Holy Spirit. "No prophecy of Scripture is a matter of one's own interpretation, for no prophecy was ever made by an act of human will, but men moved by the Holy Spirit spoke from God." ^{NASB} (2 Peter 1:20-21) The Bible is God's word! He is "upholding all things by the word of His power." (Hebrews 1:1-3) We should praise the LORD!

Psalm 148

Heaven and Earth Praise the LORD

This is the greatest psalm of praise. The LORD is praised from the heavens (verses 1-6), and he is praised from the earth (verses 7-14). All the words in the song *Hallelujah, Praise Jehovah* are from Psalm 148.

Praise the LORD!

Praise the LORD from the heavens;
Praise him in the heights.
Praise him, all his angels;
Praise him, all his hosts.
Praise him, sun and moon;
Praise him, all ye stars of light.
Praise him, ye heavens of heavens,
And ye waters above the heavens.
Let them praise the name of the LORD;
For he commanded, and they were created.
He has also established them forever and ever;
He has made a decree which shall not pass. 148:1-6

God had redeemed his people, who had been scattered among the nations. So, the psalmist calls for praise from the heavens.

John saw Jesus Christ in a vision as a resurrected Lamb that had been slain. Those around the throne of God were praising him, saying, "Thou hast redeemed us to God by thy blood out of every people and nation." John heard the voice of many angels around the throne, saying with a loud voice, "Worthy is the Lamb!" And all of God's creation in heaven and on earth were saying, 'To Him who sits on the throne and to the Lamb be blessing and honor and glory and dominion forever and ever.'" (Revelation 5:6-13) "Salvation belongs to our God who sits on the throne and to the Lamb." [NIV] (Rev. 7:9-10)

Praise the LORD from the earth,
You great sea creatures and all depths;
Fire and hail, snow and clouds;
Stormy wind, fulfilling His word;
Mountains and all hills;
Fruitful trees and all cedars;
Beasts and all cattle;
Creeping things and flying fowl;
Kings of the earth and all peoples;
Princes and all judges of the earth;
Both young men and maidens;
Old men and children.
Let them praise the name of the LORD,
For His name alone is exalted;
His glory is above the earth and heaven.
And He has exalted the horn of His people,
The praise of all His saints—
Of the children of Israel, a people near to Him. NKJV
148:7-14

From the earth, the LORD is to be praised. The design seen in nature demands a designer! An excellent building brings praise to the architect and builder; and everything that is in the earth brings praise to its Creator. "For every house is built by someone, but He who built all things is God." NKJV (Heb. 3:4) God's creation reveals his wisdom, beauty, goodness, power and judgment. In the seas are whales, sharks, dolphins, fish and other sea creatures. In the skies are beautiful clouds, sunrises and sunsets. From the skies are lightning, thunder, hail and lovely snow. Wind storms remind us that we may lose material possessions, just as God has said in his revealed word. (Haggai 1:9-11; Matthew 6:20-21)

God's grandeur, wisdom and goodness are seen in the mountains and hills, the birds that fly in the air, the wild beasts and the domesticated animals, the fruit trees for food and the cedars for wood.

The chief heads of all nations are to recognize the LORD's authority and power; and they should praise him along with administrators, governors, judges and all the people. Young men and maidens are to praise the LORD in their strength and vigor. Men and women are to praise him. Old men and little children are to praise the name of the LORD. His name means The Eternal One. His name and glory are exalted above the earth and heaven. He is before all and above all. God's people are near to him, and he gives them strength and power.

Praise ye the LORD!

Psalm 149

A New Song of Salvation

This psalm seems to be celebrating the completion of the walls of Jerusalem during the time of Nehemiah. All enemies had been defeated. The nation of Israel had been restored. God's temple and Zion's walls were rebuilt.

Praise the LORD!

Sing to the LORD a new song,
and his praise in the congregation of saints. 149:1

A special celebration calls for a new song to be sung. The godly ones were to sing God's praise in the assembly. The faithful Jews are also called saints in verses 5 and 9.

Let Israel be glad in his Maker;
Let the sons of Zion rejoice in their King. 149:2 NASB

The LORD had made the nation of Israel his holy nation. God restored the nation and his temple on Mount Zion, but it had no earthly king. The Jews were to rejoice in God, and honor him as their King. Today, Christians are the LORD's "holy nation, his own special people." (1 Peter 2:9-10) We are to rejoice in Jesus Christ our King. We are to remember **Psalm 146:3,** *Do not put your trust in mortal men, who cannot save."* Our King is the LORD! And we have come to Mount Zion … the city of the living God, the heavenly Jerusalem." (Hebrews 12:22) We are now part of the "kingdom of heaven." (Matt. 5:3; Eph. 2:4-7)

> **Let them praise his name with the dance;**
> **Let them sing praises to him with timbrel and harp.**
> **149:3**

The nation of Israel was saved when Pharaoh and his six hundred war chariots (Exodus 14:7) were destroyed in the Red Sea, "and all the women went out with tambourines and dances." (Ex.15:19-20) When the Ark of the Covenant was brought into Jerusalem, "David danced before the LORD with all his might." (2 Sam.6:14)

> **For the LORD takes pleasure in his people;**
> **He will beautify the meek with salvation.**
> **Let the saints be joyful in glory;**
> **Let them sing aloud upon their beds. 149:4-5**

Beauty may be seen in those who have been saved by the LORD. They have a pleasant disposition of gentleness and kindness because of their faith and hope. They are given inward beauty. They rejoice in the LORD always. (Philippians 4:4)

> **Let the high praises of God be in their mouth,**
> **and a two-edged sword in their hand;**
> **To execute vengeance upon the heathen,**
> **and punishment upon the people;**
> **To bind their kings with chains,**
> **and their nobles with fetters of iron.**
> **To execute upon them the judgment written;**
> **All his saints have this honor.**
>
> **Praise the LORD! 149:6-9**

Each one of the workers on the wall of Jerusalem had his sword girded at his side as he built. (Nehemiah 4:18)

This was done because the Samaritans and other nearby nations had conspired together to attack Jerusalem and stop the construction of the wall. (Neh. 3:7-9) The Jews prayed to God, and he protected them from their enemies. So, the wall was finished in fifty-two days. (Neh. 6:15)

The word of God is described as **a two-edged sword** in Hebrews 4:12 and is called **the sword of the Spirit** in Ephesians 6:17. "The LORD is my helper; I will not fear. What can man do to me?" (Hebrews 13:6) As Christians, we will suffer persecution, but "we are more than conquerors through Him who loved us." (Rom. 8:35-37)

Let's have praises to God in our mouth and the Bible in our hand! Praise the LORD!

Psalm 150

This last psalm calls upon the Jews to praise God in his temple for his mighty acts with worship prescribed in the Old Testament. (2 Chronicles 29:18-28)

> **Praise ye the LORD!**
> **Praise God in his sanctuary;**
> **Praise him in the firmament of his power.**
> **Praise him for his mighty acts;**
> **Praise him according to his excellent greatness.**
> **Praise him with the sound of the trumpet;**
> **Praise him with the psaltery and harp.**
> **Praise him with the timbrel and dance;**
> **Praise him with stringed instruments and organs.**
> **Praise him upon the loud cymbals;**
> **Praise him upon the loud sounding cymbals.**
> **Let everything that has breath praise the LORD.**
> **Praise ye the LORD! 150:1-6**

These instructions for worship are not found in the new covenant of Christ. Among the final instructions of Jesus to his apostles were, "Go, therefore, make disciples of all nations, baptizing them in the name of the Father and of the Son and of the Holy Spirit, **teaching them to observe all things that I have commanded you.**" [NKJV] (Matthew 28:19-20)

Christ's commandments are through the Scriptures inspired by the Holy Spirit (John 16:12-14; 1 Cor. 14:37). Today, we are commanded to worship God by "**singing and making melody in your heart to the Lord.**" (Ephesians 5:19) "Let the word of Christ dwell in you richly in all wisdom, teaching and admonishing one another in psalms and hymns and spiritual songs, **singing** with grace in your hearts to the Lord. And whatever you do in word or deed, do all in the name of the Lord Jesus, giving thanks to God the Father through Him." (Colossians 3:16-17) There are new psalms in the New Testament. (1 Corinthians 14:26)

God's final revelation is in Jesus Christ and his inspired apostles and prophets in the New Testament. (Ephesians 3:1-5; Hebrews 1:1-3; Luke 9:28-36) Christ through the Holy Spirit and his apostles has given to us "all things that pertain to life and godliness, through the knowledge of Him who called us by glory and virtue." (2 Peter 1:3)

Bibliography

Adam Clarke's Commentary – *Psalms.* Biblesoft

Barnes' Notes – *Psalms.* Biblesoft

Brownlow, Leroy, *Living with the Psalms.*
Fort Worth, Texas: Brownlow Publishing Company,1976.

Jamieson, Faussett and Brown Commentary, *Psalms.* Biblesoft

Keil & Delitzsch, *Commentary on the Old Testament.* Biblesoft

Limburg, James, *Psalms.* Louisville, Kentucky: Westminster John
Knox Press, 2000

M'Caw, Leslie S., *The New Bible Commentary, Psalms.*
Grand Rapids, Michigan: Wm. B. Eerdmans Publishing
Company, 1960.

Peloubet, F. N., *Peloubet's Bible Dictionary.* Philadelphia, PA:
The John C. Winston Company, 1947

Rawlinson, G., *The Pulpit Commentary, Psalms.* Grand Rapids,
Michigan: Wm. B. Eerdmans Publishing Company, 1978

Taylor, J. Herbert, *The World Book Encyclopedia,* Vol. 3, p. 418.
Chicago, Illinois: Field Enterprises Educational Corporation,
1974

Wright, George E., *The Westminster Historical Atlas to the Bible.*
Philadelphia, PA: The Westminster Press, 1956